THE CONSTITUTIONAL OPERATING SYSTEM

How a Free People Govern Power

Lisa J. Scott

A constitutional republic survives only when the people remember that government is delegated power, not sovereign authority.

The Constitutional Operating System
How a Free People Govern Power

This is a work of nonfiction. Names and identifying details have been modified where necessary to protect privacy.

ISBNs
Paperback: 978-1-971735-47-4
Hardcover: 978-1-971735-48-1
E-book: 978-1-971735-49-8

Published by
Lisa J. Scott Publishing
Dallas, Texas
www.lisajscottpublishing.com

LISA J. SCOTT
PUBLISHING

Printed in the United States of America

To America—

Not as an abstraction,
not as a slogan,
not as a perfect nation untouched by failure,

but as one of humanity's boldest attempts
to place power under law
and government under the people.

To the fragile and extraordinary idea
that liberty requires structure,
that rights are not granted by rulers,
and that free citizens are capable of governing themselves.

To those who built, defended, questioned, corrected, restrained, preserved,
and renewed this constitutional experiment across generations.

And to every citizen willing to remember
that freedom is not self-executing.

It survives only when the people do.

PREFACE

For the 250th Year

America is approaching its 250th birthday.

That is not a small milestone.

Two hundred and fifty years is long enough for a country to forget how unusual it is. Long enough for people to inherit freedoms they did not build, use rights they did not have to fight for, criticize institutions they did not have to imagine from nothing, and treat the structure beneath their lives as if it simply appeared.

But the United States did not simply appear.

It was designed.

Not perfectly. Not completely. Not without contradiction, failure, conflict, correction, and pain. But it was designed around one of the most radical premises in political history: government does not stand above the people. Government receives limited authority from the people.

That idea is still extraordinary.

The Constitution is often discussed as law, history, politics, theory, or civic memory. It is all of those things. But it is also something else.

It is an operating system.

It tells power where it may go.

It tells power where it must stop.

It divides authority before authority can concentrate.

It creates friction where ambition would prefer speed.

It recognizes rights the government did not create.

It gives change a lawful path, but not an easy shortcut.

It assumes that human beings are capable of self-government, but not that power is safe when left unbounded.

That is the genius of the design.

The Constitution was not built on naïve trust. It was built on disciplined distrust of concentrated power. It does not assume that leaders will always be wise, institutions will always be humble, courts will always be restrained, executives will always be measured, legislatures will always be principled, or citizens will always be calm.

It assumes something more realistic.

Power expands.

People panic.

Majorities can be wrong.

Emergencies can be used.

Institutions drift.

Language can be stretched.

Rights can be treated as permissions.

And government, if not restrained, can begin to mistake itself for the source of authority rather than the servant of it.

The Constitution exists because the people come first.

That is the root code.

We the People.

Not we the officials.

Not we the agencies.

Not we the experts.

Not we the temporary majority.

Not we the emergency.

We the People.

This book is written from that premise.

It is not an argument for chaos. It is not an argument against government. It is not an argument that nothing should ever change. The Constitution itself provides a method for change. But it insists that change must move through the structure, not around it.

That distinction matters.

A constitutional republic cannot survive if every generation treats the structure as an obstacle to its preferred outcome. The structure is the point. It is what allows disagreement without collapse. It is what allows correction without revolution. It is what allows power to exist without becoming absolute.

As America reaches 250 years, the question is not simply whether we celebrate the country.

The deeper question is whether we still understand the system.

Do we understand what was built?

Do we understand why it was built that way?

Do we understand what happens when the branches blur, rights are reframed as favors, emergencies become habits, or citizens become spectators?

Do we understand that freedom is not self-maintaining?

This book is an attempt to look beneath the noise.

Not at the daily fight.

Not at the personalities.

Not at the emotional weather of the moment.

But at the operating system itself.

The Constitution is not merely old paper.

It is a restraint system for power.

It is an architecture of liberty.

It is a legal memory of what happens when government forgets its place.

And at its core, it still says something simple and profound:

The government serves the people.

The people do not belong to the government.

That is worth remembering at 250 years.

That is worth teaching.

That is worth protecting.

TABLE OF CONTENTS

PART IV — THE FAILURE MODES

PART V — THE AMENDMENT DISCIPLINE

PART VI — CITIZENSHIP AS SYSTEM STEWARDSHIP

DIAGRAMS AND ILLUSTRATION

INTRODUCTION

THE SYSTEM BENEATH THE COUNTRY

Every country has a surface.

Flags. Buildings. Elections. Leaders. Courts. Speeches. Headlines. Conflicts. Symbols. Arguments. Moments of pride. Moments of shame. Moments when the country seems unified. Moments when it appears to be coming apart.

That is the visible country.

But beneath the visible country is another country.

A structure.

A system.

A design for how power is supposed to move, where it is supposed to stop, and who it is supposed to serve.

That system is the Constitution.

The Constitution is often treated as an artifact. Something old. Something framed. Something quoted on holidays, debated in courtrooms, invoked in campaigns, and taught in fragments to students who are rarely shown the whole architecture.

But the Constitution was not written merely to be admired.

It was written to function.

It is not a relic.

It is an operating system.

An operating system does not exist to decorate a device. It exists to make the device work. It sets permissions. It limits access. It assigns functions. It defines what may run, what may not run, and what happens when something attempts to exceed its authority.

The Constitution does the same thing for government.

It tells Congress what kind of power it has.

It tells the President what kind of power he has.

It tells the courts what kind of power they have.

It divides authority so that no single part of government can become the whole.

It recognizes rights that stand outside the government's ownership.

It gives the people mechanisms for correction, representation, amendment, and resistance to overreach.

It is not just a statement of ideals.

It is a structure for restraining power.

That matters because power does not remain still.

Power moves.

Power accumulates.

Power justifies itself.

Power uses emergencies.

Power borrows the language of safety, fairness, necessity, efficiency, compassion, and progress. Sometimes those words are sincere. Sometimes they are not. But the Constitution was designed with an understanding that good intentions are not enough to protect a free people.

A government can do harm while claiming to help.

A majority can violate liberty while claiming to represent democracy.

An institution can exceed its proper role while claiming expertise.

A court can reinterpret what should have been amended.

An executive can act as if urgency removes limits.

A legislature can delegate what it should have debated.

A bureaucracy can become powerful enough that citizens no longer know who made the rule, where the authority came from, or how to object.

This is why structure matters more than mood.

Mood changes.

Fear rises.

Anger spreads.

Movements gain force.

Leaders become popular.

Institutions become fashionable or hated.

Public opinion moves like weather across the surface of the country.

But constitutional structure is not supposed to move with the weather.

It is supposed to hold.

It is supposed to remain visible when the public is emotional, when leaders are ambitious, when institutions are confident, and when citizens are tempted to trade limits for outcomes.

The Constitution is not there only when people agree with it.

It is there when they do not.

It is not there only when the process produces the preferred result.

It is there when the process blocks the preferred result.

That is when the system proves whether it is real.

A constitutional republic cannot be governed by mood without eventually losing its shape. If every crisis becomes a reason to bypass the structure, the structure is no longer the rule. It becomes decoration. If every desired outcome justifies a shortcut, the people are no longer governing power. Power is governing the people through emotion.

The American system begins somewhere else.

It begins with source authority.

"We the People."

Those are not ceremonial words.

They are the root code.

The Constitution does not begin with the government granting rights to the people. It begins with the people ordaining and establishing the Constitution.

That order matters.

The people come first.

The government comes second.

Government is not the source. Government is the recipient of delegated power. It has authority only because authority has been given to it, limited by written structure, divided among branches, constrained by rights, and subject to correction.

This is one of the most important ideas in the American constitutional system: the government is not sovereign over the people in the way a monarch was sovereign over subjects.

The people are sovereign.

Government serves by delegation.

That does not mean government is unnecessary. The Constitution creates a government because ordered liberty requires form. A free people still need law, courts, defense, representation, administration, and public order. Freedom does not mean the absence of structure.

Freedom requires the right structure.

Too little structure can produce chaos.

Too much power can produce tyranny.

The Constitution attempts to solve that tension.

It gives government enough authority to function, but not enough authority to become the master of the people.

It grants power, then restrains it.

It creates offices, then limits them.

It allows change, then disciplines the method.

It permits disagreement, then gives disagreement a lawful system through which to move.

It does not assume that the people will always agree. It assumes they will not. The system was built for disagreement. It was built for ambition. It was built for competing interests, regional differences, institutional conflict, and human imperfection.

That is why friction exists inside the design.

Friction is not always failure.

Sometimes friction is the system working.

When a bill is difficult to pass, that may be frustrating. But it may also mean the system is requiring deliberation.

When branches resist each other, that may appear inefficient. But it may also mean power is not moving unchecked.

When states differ from one another, that may seem disorderly. But it may also mean authority remains closer to the people.

When amendments are difficult, that may feel outdated. But it may also mean permanent structural change requires serious agreement.

The Constitution is not designed for constant emotional satisfaction.

It is designed for durable self-government.

That is a different standard.

Self-government requires more than voting. It requires memory. It requires restraint. It requires citizens who understand that not every political desire should become law, not every law is constitutional, not every emergency justifies expansion, and not every institution should be trusted simply because it speaks in the language of expertise.

A free people must know the system beneath the country.

Otherwise, they can be moved by whatever is loudest on the surface.

They can be taught to confuse government action with justice.

They can be taught to confuse resistance with extremism.

They can be taught to confuse constitutional limits with inconvenience.

They can be taught to confuse rights with permissions.

They can be taught to confuse the temporary will of power with the enduring authority of the people.

This book is an attempt to return to the system.

Not as nostalgia.

Not as performance.

Not as partisan language.

But as structure.

The Constitution is not perfect because no human design is perfect. It emerged from history, compromise, conflict, blindness, wisdom, and correction. It has been amended. It has been tested. It has been violated. It has been defended. It has been stretched, ignored, invoked, and restored in different ways across generations.

But its central architecture remains extraordinary.

Power is not unlimited.

Rights are not favors.

Government is not the source.

The people are not subjects.

Change is possible, but must move through lawful form.

The system exists so that power can be governed.

That is the country beneath the country.

And if America is to remain free, that system must be understood not only by lawyers, judges, politicians, and scholars.

It must be understood by the people.

Because the people are the source.

THE CONSTITUTIONAL OPERATING SYSTEM

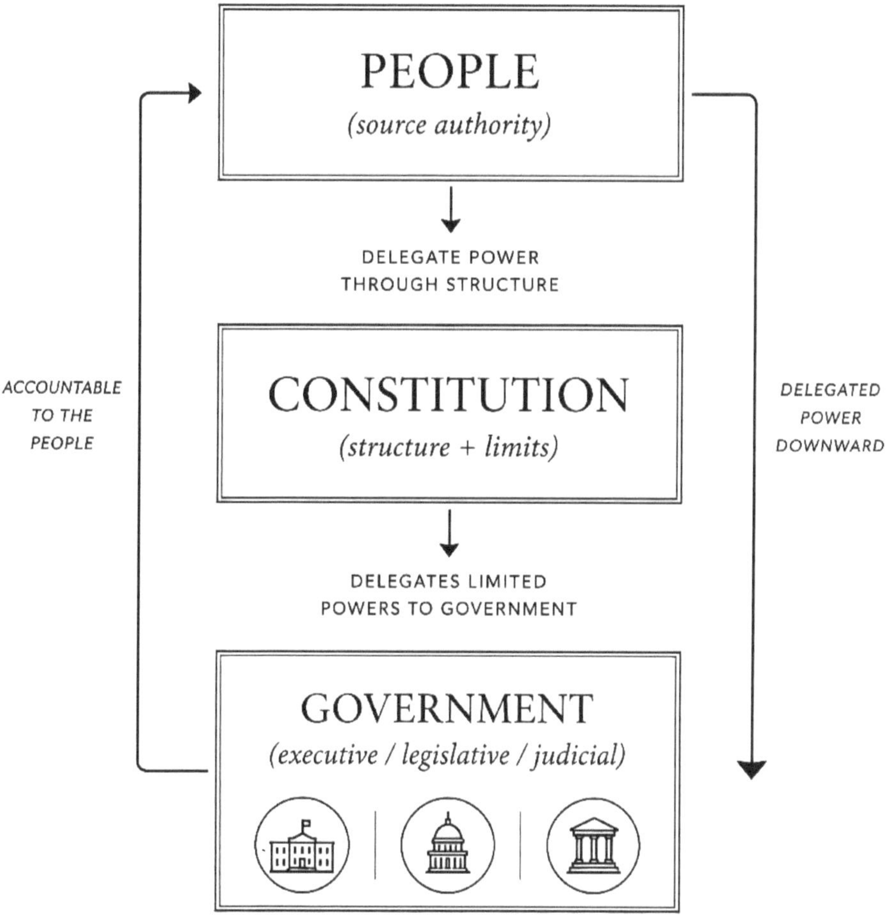

↓ POWER FLOWS DOWNWARD:
The People delegate limited powers through the Constitution.

↑ ACCOUNTABILITY FLOWS UPWARD:
Government is accountable to the People.

PART I —

THE SOURCE CODE

Before power can be governed, authority must be traced to its source.

1

The People Are the Root Authority

The first words of the Constitution are not about government.

They are about the people.

"We the People."

Those three words establish the entire logic of the American system.

Not we the rulers.

Not we the officials.

Not we the states.

Not we the military.

Not we the experts.

Not we the court.

We the People.

That order is not symbolic decoration. It is the foundation of constitutional authority itself.

The Constitution does not present government as a force that grants freedom downward to the population. It presents the people as the source from which government authority rises upward.

That distinction changes everything.

In older systems of rule, authority often flowed from the top down. Kings ruled by bloodline. Monarchs claimed divine right. Subjects existed beneath the state. Rights were temporary allowances that could be narrowed, revoked, suspended, or ignored depending on the ruler, the crisis, or the political climate.

The American constitutional system attempted something radically different.

The people themselves were sovereign.

Government would exist by consent.

Authority would be delegated.

Power would be limited.

And the structure itself would remain subordinate to the source that created it.

This idea is so deeply woven into American civic language that many people no longer stop to notice how revolutionary it was.

A government that derives "its just powers from the consent of the governed" is fundamentally different from a government that assumes ownership over the population.

Consent is not the same thing as permission.

Permission flows downward from a superior authority.

Consent flows upward from the people themselves.

That distinction matters because it defines the relationship between citizen and state.

A citizen is not a subject waiting to be managed.

A citizen is part of the sovereign body from which governmental legitimacy is derived.

This does not mean every individual gets everything he or she wants. Constitutional self-government still requires law, elections, process, compromise, and limits. A free people cannot function without structure. But the legitimacy of that structure rests on the principle that authority originates with the people, not apart from them.

That is why constitutional systems place such importance on representation, elections, amendment procedures, due process, and limits on state power. Those mechanisms are not merely administrative. They reflect a deeper assumption: government is accountable because it is not the owner of the people.

It serves them.

This is one of the most important mental distinctions in the constitutional operating system.

Government serves.

It does not own.

That line can begin to blur slowly over time.

A government may begin by administering law but gradually behave as though it possesses the population rather than represents it. Citizens may begin to see themselves less as self-governing participants and more as managed recipients. Rights may begin to feel conditional. Speech may begin to feel permitted rather than protected. Institutions may begin to speak as though disagreement itself is disobedience.

This is how constitutional cultures weaken—not always through dramatic collapse, but through subtle inversion of the relationship between citizen and power.

When people begin to fear the government more than the government fears violating the Constitution, the balance has shifted.

The American system was intentionally designed to prevent that inversion.

Public officials swear an oath not to themselves, not to a ruler, and not even to a political party. They swear an oath to the Constitution because the Constitution is the framework that limits their authority and reminds them that they are exercising delegated power.

Delegated power is temporary.

Delegated power is conditional.

Delegated power is bounded.

No officeholder owns the office.

No branch owns the country.

No institution owns the citizen.

The authority exists only within constitutional limits.

This is why constitutional literacy matters so deeply. A people who forget where authority originates become vulnerable to manipulation by institutions that slowly redefine themselves as the source rather than the servant of power.

Over time, language itself can change.

Citizens become "users."

Rights become "privileges."

Freedoms become "access."

Dissent becomes "risk."

Compliance becomes confused with virtue.

And government slowly shifts from steward to manager of the population.

The Constitution stands against that shift.

Its opening words are a declaration of source authority.

"We the People" means the country does not belong to its officials.

It means the state is not sovereign over human dignity.

It means the citizen is not merely an economic unit, demographic category, or administrative subject.

It means the government derives legitimacy only through lawful delegation from the people themselves.

That principle also explains why constitutional limits matter even when people strongly support a particular policy or leader.

If government authority is derived from the people through constitutional structure, then no temporary majority can simply bypass the structure because it desires a certain outcome. Otherwise, the people are no longer governing through law. They are governing through impulse.

The Constitution restrains that temptation.

It says there are lawful methods.

There are enumerated powers.

There are rights that remain protected even when unpopular.

There are procedures for amendment.

There are boundaries that cannot simply disappear because the public mood changes.

That restraint protects everyone, including future minorities, future dissenters, and future generations who may inherit a government far more aggressive than the one people temporarily trusted.

The founders understood something enduring about human nature: power often expands most easily when citizens believe it is being used for good purposes.

That is why liberty cannot depend entirely on trust.

It requires structure.

A constitutional republic depends on citizens remembering the difference between authority and ownership.

Government possesses authority within lawful limits.

It does not possess the people.

The people are the source.

The people are the sovereign body.

And the Constitution exists to ensure that delegated power never forgets where it came from.

2

A System Built from Distrust of Power

The Constitution was not built because the founders trusted power.

It was built because they did not.

That is one of the most important things to understand about the American constitutional operating system. It was not designed around the assumption that human beings in office would remain humble, restrained, wise, or virtuous once given authority.

It was designed around the opposite assumption.

Power tempts.

Power expands.

Power explains itself.

Power believes its own necessity.

Power prefers fewer obstacles.

Power does not usually announce itself as tyranny at the beginning. It often arrives as order, efficiency, security, fairness, expertise, emergency, compassion, or national need.

That is why constitutional structure matters.

The founders had lived under a system where distant power could reach into ordinary life without adequate consent or representation. They understood that authority concentrated far away from the people could become indifferent to the people. They understood that centralized power could begin to treat citizens not as the source of legitimacy, but as objects to be governed, taxed, managed, punished, or corrected.

Their answer was not to eliminate government.

Their answer was to bind it.

A constitutional republic is not anarchy. It is not the absence of power. It is ordered power under law.

The founders knew government was necessary. A nation needed defense. It needed courts. It needed commerce. It needed a framework for union. It needed the ability to act. But it also needed something just as important: a system that made government dangerous to itself before it became dangerous to the people.

That is the genius of divided power.

The American system does not place all authority in one person, one chamber, one court, one agency, or one temporary majority. It divides power before power can fully gather itself.

Legislative power is separated from executive power.

Executive power is separated from judicial power.

Federal power is separated from state power.

Public authority is restrained by individual rights.

Majorities are restrained by constitutional boundaries.

Even change itself is restrained by amendment procedure.

This is not inefficiency by accident.

It is friction by design.

The Constitution assumes that liberty cannot survive if power moves too easily in one direction. A government that can act without resistance may appear effective for a time, especially when people agree with what it is doing. But the same smooth machinery can later be used for purposes those same people fear.

That is why liberty requires limits even when the cause seems good.

Especially then.

The temptation is always to say that limits should apply to the other side, the bad leader, the corrupt institution, the unpopular movement, the dangerous idea, the crisis we disapprove of. But constitutional limits are not meaningful if they only apply when they are convenient. The entire point of a constitutional system is that limits remain when passion rises.

A free people cannot depend on the character of whoever happens to hold power.

They need structure that outlasts personality.

They need boundaries that remain in place when the crowd is angry.

They need procedures that continue to matter when the outcome is emotionally charged.

They need rights that do not disappear when dissent is unpopular.

They need branches that can resist each other.

They need courts that interpret rather than rule.

They need executives who execute rather than command without limit.

They need legislatures that deliberate rather than delegate their function away.

They need states that retain meaningful authority.

They need citizens who understand that freedom is not protected by trusting power, but by governing it.

This is why the Constitution begins from a sober view of human nature. It does not assume that power becomes safe because it is held by educated people, elected people, credentialed people, popular people, patriotic people, or people who use the correct moral language.

Power is still power.

It must be limited before it can be trusted.

The founders feared concentrated authority because concentrated authority changes the relationship between government and citizen. When power gathers into one place, the citizen has fewer points of resistance. The law becomes harder to challenge. Decisions become less transparent. Accountability becomes distant. The people can no longer see clearly where authority originated, who exercised it, or how to correct it.

A system with divided power gives citizens more than one door through which to seek protection.

If Congress overreaches, courts may check it.

If the executive exceeds authority, Congress may resist.

If the federal government goes too far, states may object.

If a majority tramples rights, constitutional protections may intervene.

If the structure itself needs change, the amendment process provides a lawful path.

The purpose is not paralysis.

The purpose is protection.

Liberty is not preserved by making government powerless. It is preserved by making government accountable, limited, divided, and answerable to the source of its authority.

That source is the people.

A system built from distrust of power is not a cynical system. It is a realistic one.

It understands that even good people can misuse authority.

It understands that institutions can drift.

It understands that emergencies can stretch language.

It understands that temporary solutions can become permanent habits.

It understands that convenience is often the enemy of liberty.

It understands that the desire to "get things done" can become a justification for bypassing the very structure that keeps a free people free.

The Constitution does not trust power to restrain itself.

So it separates power.

It slows power.

It exposes power.

It makes power answerable to other power.

It leaves rights outside the ordinary reach of political appetite.

And it makes the government operate within a system it did not invent and does not own.

This is why the Constitution can feel frustrating.

It is supposed to.

It frustrates rulers.

It frustrates majorities.

It frustrates movements.

It frustrates emergencies.

It frustrates anyone who wants power to move faster than lawful structure permits.

But that frustration is not always a defect.

Sometimes frustration is liberty breathing.

Sometimes delay is protection.

Sometimes resistance is the system doing its work.

Sometimes the obstacle is the safeguard.

A government that never encounters limits is not serving a free people. It is becoming something else.

The founders understood this. They knew liberty could not be preserved by merely declaring rights or celebrating independence. Freedom needed architecture. It needed walls. It needed locked doors. It needed separate rooms. It needed procedures. It needed oaths. It needed courts. It needed elections. It needed states. It needed written limits.

It needed distrust built into the design.

Not distrust of America.

Distrust of unchecked power.

That distinction is essential.

To distrust concentrated power is not to hate government. It is to understand government's proper place.

Government has a role.

Government has duties.

Government has legitimate authority.

But it does not have unlimited authority.

It does not own the people.

It does not stand above the Constitution.

It does not get to become larger simply because it claims necessity.

The constitutional operating system was built to keep power from forgetting that.

Before power expands, it must be divided.

Before it acts, it must be authorized.

Before it reaches the citizen, it must pass through law.

Before it claims permanence, it must face consent.

That is the architecture of ordered liberty.

That is the discipline beneath the design.

And that is why a free people should not be offended by constitutional limits.

They should recognize them as one of the greatest protections they have.

3

Written Structure as Protection

A written Constitution matters because memory is not enough.

Custom is not enough.

Tradition is not enough.

Good intentions are not enough.

A free people need something more durable than the mood of the moment and more stable than the character of whoever happens to hold office. They need a structure that can be read, invoked, taught, challenged, defended, and returned to when power begins to drift.

That is what a written Constitution provides.

It makes the rules visible.

It puts authority into language.

It gives the people something to point to when government exceeds its place.

Without written structure, power can become elastic. Limits can become vague. Rights can become dependent on institutional memory, political habit, or judicial preference. The boundary between lawful authority and convenient expansion becomes easier to blur.

A written Constitution creates a fixed reference point.

Not because every clause will interpret itself.

Not because language removes every dispute.

Not because human beings will always agree.

But because written structure prevents power from becoming the only interpreter of its own reach.

The words matter.

The order matters.

The limits matter.

The procedures matter.

The fact that the structure exists outside the temporary officeholder matters.

A president did not write the office into existence.

A Congress does not own its own powers.

A court does not stand above the text it interprets.

An agency does not become lawful simply because it is useful.

The written Constitution is the architecture they all operate within.

That architecture must exist before the emergency.

Rules written during panic are rarely rules of restraint.

When people are afraid, they often want speed more than structure. They want action more than deliberation. They want protection more than process. They may even begin to see constitutional limits as an obstacle to safety, progress, justice, or necessity.

But emergencies are exactly when written limits matter most.

It is easy to honor structure when nothing is at stake.

It is easy to praise liberty in calm conditions.

It is easy to respect procedure when the outcome is not urgent.

The test comes when people are frightened, angry, wounded, or convinced that history requires immediate action.

That is when power asks for exceptions.

That is when leaders speak of necessity.

That is when institutions argue that the usual rules are too slow.

That is when citizens are tempted to surrender limits in exchange for reassurance.

And that is when a written Constitution must stand.

Rules before emergencies.

Not because emergencies are imaginary.

Not because danger is never real.

Not because government should never act.

But because crisis is the oldest justification for expansion of power.

A government that can define an emergency, expand its own authority, suspend limits, and then decide when the emergency is over has already moved outside the discipline of constitutional design.

The Constitution does not exist for peaceful moments only.

It exists for pressure.

It exists for fear.

It exists for conflict.

It exists for the moment when the majority wants speed, the executive wants reach, the legislature wants escape from responsibility, the court wants to solve what was not submitted to the people, or the bureaucracy wants to convert temporary authority into permanent administration.

Written structure interrupts that movement.

It asks: where is the authority?

Who was given this power?

What branch is acting?

What limit applies?

What process was followed?

What right is being touched?

What remedy exists?

Those questions are not technicalities.

They are safeguards.

A free people should be wary when constitutional questions are dismissed as technicalities. A technicality is often what a limit looks like to someone who wants to pass through it.

Clarity protects.

Ambiguity serves power.

When limits are unclear, power can stretch them.

When rights are vague, institutions can redefine them.

When authority is assumed rather than granted, government can grow without ever admitting that it has crossed a line.

Clarity does not solve every problem, but it gives citizens a place to stand.

It allows the people to distinguish between government acting within its lawful role and government simply acting because it can.

It allows disagreement to become specific.

It allows resistance to become grounded.

It allows courts, legislators, states, citizens, and future generations to return to the same source.

This is why constitutional language should not be treated casually. When words are stretched too far, the system loses shape. When terms are transformed to fit desired outcomes, the written Constitution becomes less like a boundary and more like raw material.

That is dangerous.

A constitution that means whatever power needs it to mean does not restrain power.

It serves power.

The protection lies in the fact that the words are not supposed to belong to the moment. They are not supposed to belong to the official currently interpreting them. They are not supposed to belong to the loudest movement or the strongest institution.

They belong to the constitutional order.

They belong to the people who ratified the structure, amended it through lawful means, and remain bound together by it.

This does not mean interpretation is unnecessary. A written Constitution must be applied to circumstances the framers could not have imagined. New technologies emerge. New conflicts arise. New forms of power develop. The country changes.

But application is not the same as abandonment.

Interpretation is not the same as replacement.

Adaptation is not the same as rewriting without consent.

A written Constitution gives change a discipline. It allows the system to respond to new conditions while still requiring power to remain tethered to text, structure, history, and lawful amendment.

That tether is protection.

A country without a written constitutional boundary is more vulnerable to drift. A country with a written Constitution is not automatically safe, but it has a visible instrument of correction. Citizens can read it. Lawyers can argue from it. Judges can be measured against it. Legislators can be confronted with it. Executives can be limited by it. Teachers can pass it down. Movements can be judged by whether they honor or bypass it.

The written form matters because it makes betrayal harder to hide.

It makes overreach easier to name.

It makes civic memory portable.

It allows each generation to inherit not just stories about freedom, but the operating structure through which freedom is supposed to be preserved.

The Constitution is not protected merely because it is written.

It is protected when the people treat the writing as binding.

That is the burden of a constitutional republic.

The text must not become decoration.

The structure must not become a slogan.

The clauses must not become museum language.

Written limits matter only when citizens insist that government remain inside them.

The Constitution protects because it is external to the appetite of power.

It stands outside the emergency.

It stands outside the election cycle.

It stands outside institutional ambition.

It stands outside the personal virtue of leaders.

It says: this is the structure.

This is where power begins.

This is where power ends.

This is what government may do.

This is what government may not do.

This is how change must occur.

That kind of clarity is not restrictive to a free people.

It is liberating.

Because when power is bounded, citizens can breathe.

When authority is written, citizens can question.

When rights are named, citizens can assert them.

When procedures are visible, citizens can demand that they be followed.

When government forgets its place, the written Constitution reminds it.

A written Constitution matters because freedom cannot depend on trust alone.

It needs structure.

It needs memory.

It needs language.

It needs limits that remain legible under pressure.

It needs rules before emergencies.

It needs clarity as a safeguard.

And it needs a people willing to say: the system still matters, especially now.

PART II —

THE ARCHITECTURE OF LIMITED POWER

Liberty survives when power is divided before it can become whole.

4

ENUMERATED POWERS

Limited government does not mean weak government.

It means defined government.

That distinction is essential to the constitutional operating system. The Constitution does not create a national government and then leave it free to discover its own reach. It creates a government of assigned powers, structured functions, and written boundaries.

The federal government may act where authority has been granted to it.

It may not simply act because the issue is important.

It may not simply act because the public wants action.

It may not simply act because experts believe action would be useful.

It may not simply act because a crisis has created urgency.

It may not simply act because government power seems like the fastest tool available.

In the constitutional design, importance is not the same as authority.

This is the logic of enumerated powers.

To enumerate is to list, to name, to specify. The Constitution gives the federal government certain powers. Those powers are real. They are significant. They allow the government to tax, spend, regulate commerce, provide for national defense, establish courts, coin money, declare war, conduct foreign affairs, and perform other functions necessary to the operation of a nation.

But the list matters.

The fact that powers are named means they are not assumed to be unlimited.

A government of enumerated powers is a government that must answer the threshold question: where does this authority come from?

That question is one of the most important safeguards in the entire constitutional system.

Before asking whether a policy is popular, efficient, compassionate, modern, or desirable, the constitutional question is more basic:

Was this power granted?

That question disciplines government.

It forces authority to identify its source.

It prevents power from treating usefulness as permission.

It reminds public officials that they are not operating from general ownership over the country, but from delegated authority within a written structure.

Delegated authority is authority given for a purpose and bounded by the terms of the delegation.

Assumed authority is different.

Assumed authority begins with the government's desire to act and then searches for justification afterward. It treats silence as permission. It treats need as power. It treats public pressure as authorization. It treats institutional confidence as legitimacy.

That is not the constitutional order.

In the constitutional operating system, government does not begin with total power and then give portions back to the people.

It begins with limited power delegated by the people.

The people retain what they have not delegated.

This is why enumerated powers matter so deeply. They preserve the direction of authority. Power flows from the people into government for specific purposes. It does not flow from government over the people by default.

When that order is forgotten, government expands without necessarily admitting that it has changed character.

The expansion may appear reasonable at first. A problem arises. The problem is real. Citizens are worried. Leaders promise action. Agencies develop programs. Courts tolerate broader interpretations. Congress writes broad language. Executives use flexible authority. Each step may be defended as necessary.

But over time, assumed authority begins to replace delegated authority.

The question quietly changes.

Instead of asking, "Where does the Constitution grant this power?" government begins asking, "Why shouldn't we do this?"

That reversal is profound.

A government of enumerated powers must justify action by reference to granted authority.

A government of assumed powers expects citizens to justify why government should stop.

The burden shifts.

And when the burden shifts, liberty shifts with it.

Limits matter because they decide who must explain himself.

In a free constitutional system, government should have to explain the source of its power before it acts against the citizen. The citizen should not have to prove that freedom exists in the spaces government has not yet chosen to regulate.

Freedom is the default.

Government authority is the exception that must be grounded.

That is the architecture of limited power.

This does not mean the federal government has no role in national problems. It means its role must be constitutionally authorized. The Constitution was created because the Articles of Confederation had left the national government too weak for certain national needs. The framers understood that a functioning union required real federal authority.

But they also understood that giving government power without limits would recreate the very danger the Revolution had resisted.

So the Constitution strengthened government and restrained it at the same time.

That balance is difficult.

It was meant to be.

A national government needs enough authority to govern a nation, but not so much authority that every issue becomes federal, every problem becomes centralized, and every citizen becomes dependent on distant decision-makers.

Enumerated powers protect that balance.

They keep the federal government from becoming a general-purpose authority over all human life.

They preserve space for states.

They preserve space for local communities.

They preserve space for private ordering.

They preserve space for families, churches, associations, businesses, schools, property owners, and individual conscience.

They preserve space for the citizen to live without constant federal supervision.

A society does not remain free merely because elections occur. A society remains free when power is limited between elections.

That is why limits matter even when voters like the people currently in power. Constitutional structure cannot depend on temporary trust. The same power granted to solve one favored problem may later be used by different officials for purposes the original supporters never imagined.

Power does not retire when its preferred administration leaves office.

It remains in the system.

Every expansion becomes available to the next person who holds the tool.

This is why constitutional limits are not partisan protections. They are structural protections. They protect the people from power regardless of who controls it.

An enumerated power is a gate.

It asks power to show its credentials before entering.

Without that gate, government can become a machine that converts every public concern into federal authority.

That may feel satisfying in the short term. It may create the appearance of responsiveness. But it also weakens the discipline of self-government. Citizens begin to look upward for solutions that may belong closer to them. Congress begins to write broader laws. Agencies begin to fill gaps. Courts begin to defer. Presidents begin to act. The federal system begins to tilt.

The result is not always sudden tyranny.

Often, it is administrative dependency.

Distance grows between citizen and decision. Accountability becomes harder to locate. The people know they are being governed, but they may no longer know by whom, under what authority, or how to correct it.

Enumerated powers resist that drift.

They make government return to source.

They require law to remain connected to constitutional permission.

They remind each branch that it cannot enlarge itself by desire.

Congress cannot legislate merely because something should be done.

The executive cannot act merely because something must be done quickly.

The courts cannot approve authority merely because the outcome seems beneficial.

Agencies cannot govern merely because the details are complex.

The threshold remains:

Was the power granted?

That question protects the people because it refuses to let government become the measure of its own authority.

It also protects constitutional legitimacy. A government that acts within its granted powers can command obedience through law. A government that repeatedly acts beyond its powers may gain compliance, but it loses legitimacy.

Compliance and legitimacy are not the same thing.

People may comply because they are afraid, exhausted, confused, busy, dependent, or outmatched.

Legitimacy requires something deeper.

It requires lawful authority.

The Constitution is concerned with lawful authority because a free people cannot be ruled by mere force, habit, expertise, or administrative convenience. They must be governed through powers they have actually granted.

This is why the idea of enumerated powers belongs near the center of the constitutional operating system.

It is not a minor legal doctrine.

It is a structural statement about sovereignty.

The government has only the power it has been given.

The people retain the rest.

That principle is one of the clearest ways the Constitution keeps government in its proper place.

It does not deny that problems exist.

It does not deny that government has important work to do.

It does not deny that the country changes.

It simply insists that power must remain authorized.

Because when government can assume authority rather than receive it, the people are no longer the source.

They become the object.

Enumerated powers prevent that inversion.

They keep the government from treating the country as something it owns.

They keep public power inside written boundaries.

They keep freedom from becoming whatever remains after government finishes expanding.

And they remind every generation of the first principle beneath the structure:

Government serves by delegation.

It does not rule by assumption.

5

SEPARATION OF POWERS

The Constitution does not merely limit power by naming it.

It limits power by separating it.

This is one of the central design decisions of the American constitutional operating system. Power is not placed into one office, one body, one institution, or one class of decision-makers. It is divided into branches, each with a different function, a different role, and a different relationship to the people.

Legislative.

Executive.

Judicial.

Each branch has power.

But no branch has all power.

That is the point.

The legislative branch makes law.

The executive branch carries out law.

The judicial branch interprets law and resolves disputes under law.

Those distinctions sound simple, but they are one of the most important protections in the entire constitutional structure. A free people cannot remain free if the same hands that make the law also enforce the law and then decide what the law means when challenged.

That concentration would collapse the system into itself.

The Constitution separates functions because function is power.

To make law is power.

To execute law is power.

To interpret law is power.

If one institution holds all three, it does not merely govern. It commands.

The separation of powers keeps authority from becoming whole in one place.

It forces power to move through structure.

It requires different branches to participate in different ways.

It creates accountability by making roles visible.

When Congress legislates, the people can see who made the law.

When the President executes, the people can see who administered it.

When courts interpret, the people can see how legal disputes were resolved.

The design is not perfect. No human system is. But the separation makes abuse harder to hide because power must reveal which function it is exercising.

This matters because confusion begins when functions blur.

When Congress refuses to legislate clearly and instead passes broad authority to agencies, the legislative function begins to dissolve into administration.

When the executive uses emergency power, executive orders, enforcement discretion, or regulatory pressure to create outcomes that Congress did not enact, execution begins to look like legislation.

When courts interpret constitutional or statutory language so expansively that they effectively create new policy, interpretation begins to look like lawmaking.

When agencies write rules, enforce rules, and adjudicate violations of their own rules, all three functions begin to gather inside the administrative state.

That is where constitutional confusion begins.

And confusion serves power.

A citizen can resist a law when he knows who passed it.

He can challenge enforcement when he knows who enforced it.

He can appeal a judgment when he knows who decided it.

But when functions blur, accountability becomes foggy. The citizen no longer knows where the decision truly came from. Was it Congress? Was it the agency? Was it the President? Was it a court? Was it guidance? Was it interpretation? Was it enforcement discretion? Was it policy hidden inside process?

Blurred power is harder to see.

And what is harder to see is harder to govern.

The separation of powers protects liberty by making authority traceable.

It says: this branch does this.

This branch does not do everything.

The legislative branch is closest to the people in the lawmaking function. Members of Congress stand for election. They debate. They vote. They are supposed to bear responsibility for the laws they impose. That responsibility is not always comfortable. It should not be. Making law for a free people should require deliberation, exposure, disagreement, and accountability.

If Congress gives away too much of its lawmaking function, the people lose visibility. Rules still come, but they no longer arrive through the clearest form of representative lawmaking. They emerge from offices, agencies, procedures, and expert bodies farther from ordinary electoral correction.

The executive branch exists to carry out the law, not to become the lawgiver.

The President has significant constitutional authority. The executive must enforce law, protect the country, conduct foreign affairs within constitutional bounds, and lead the administrative machinery of government. But energy in the executive was never meant to become ownership of the system.

Execution is not permission to rewrite.

Urgency is not permission to legislate.

Leadership is not permission to bypass the people's representatives.

The judicial branch has its own crucial role. Courts protect the rule of law by resolving cases and controversies, interpreting legal text, and ensuring that constitutional limits are not merely ornamental. Judicial independence matters because courts must sometimes stand against popular pressure or government overreach.

But interpretation is not the same as authorship.

A court that treats interpretation as the power to revise the constitutional structure risks becoming a branch of policy rather than judgment. When that happens, the people are no longer governed by laws they can amend through constitutional process. They are governed by meanings that shift through judicial preference.

Each branch becomes dangerous when it forgets its function.

Congress becomes dangerous when it avoids responsibility.

The executive becomes dangerous when it mistakes action for authority.

The judiciary becomes dangerous when it confuses interpretation with creation.

The administrative state becomes dangerous when it absorbs the functions of all three.

Separation of powers exists because liberty requires boundaries not only between government and citizen, but inside government itself.

Power must be kept from fusing.

The Constitution does not trust a single institution to hold the whole design. It does not assume that elected officials are safe because they were elected. It does not assume that executives are safe because they are decisive. It does not assume that judges are safe because they are educated. It does not assume that agencies are safe because they are specialized.

It assumes power must be structured.

This is why the separation of powers can feel slow.

It requires law to be made through one process, enforced through another, and judged through another. It creates tension. It produces conflict. It frustrates officials who want cleaner lines of command. It frustrates citizens who want faster results.

But speed is not the highest value in a constitutional republic.

Legitimacy matters more than speed.

Accountability matters more than convenience.

Liberty matters more than administrative elegance.

A system where the same authority can declare the rule, enforce the rule, interpret the rule, punish violation of the rule, and then defend its own action as necessary is efficient only in the way machinery is efficient.

It may move quickly.

But it is no longer self-government in the constitutional sense.

SEPARATION OF POWERS

Three Independent Branches.
Shared Purpose. Limited Power.

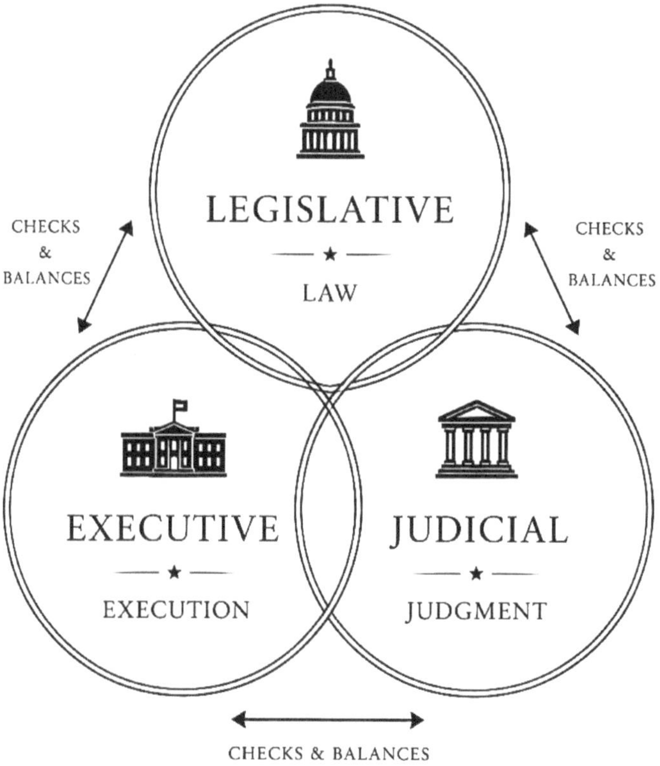

No branch is supreme.
Each is limited.
Each is accountable.
Together they protect liberty.

6

Checks and Balances

Separation alone is not enough.

Power must not only be divided.

It must be made to resist itself.

That is the purpose of checks and balances.

The Constitution does not merely place legislative, executive, and judicial powers in different branches and then hope each branch behaves. It gives the branches ways to limit one another. It builds tension into the design so that no branch can easily become final, complete, or unanswerable.

Ambition checks ambition.

That phrase captures one of the deepest insights in the constitutional operating system. The framers did not assume that officials would restrain themselves out of humility. They understood that people who hold power often want to preserve it, expand it, defend it, and justify it.

So the system uses that reality.

It does not pretend ambition disappears in public office.

It channels ambition against ambition.

Congress has powers the President does not have.

The President has powers Congress does not have.

The courts have powers neither political branch can fully control.

Each branch has its own source of authority, its own institutional interest, and its own constitutional role. When one branch reaches too far, another branch has reason and means to push back.

This is not accidental conflict.

It is designed resistance.

The veto is a check.

Impeachment is a check.

Judicial review is a check.

Senate confirmation is a check.

Congressional oversight is a check.

The power of the purse is a check.

Elections are a check.

Federalism is a check.

Rights are a check.

The amendment process is a check.

The people themselves are the ultimate check.

The system is full of friction because liberty requires more than trust.

No branch is trusted alone.

That is the discipline beneath the architecture.

The legislative branch may represent the people, but representation does not make Congress unlimited.

The executive may need energy and decisiveness, but energy does not make the President supreme.

The judiciary may interpret law, but interpretation does not make courts sovereign.

Each branch is necessary.

Each branch is dangerous.

Each branch must be limited by the others.

This is one reason the Constitution can feel frustrating to those who want immediate results. A bill may pass one chamber and fail in another. A President may want to act but need congressional authorization. Congress may pass a law that courts later find unconstitutional. Courts may issue decisions that require political response through legislation or amendment. Agencies may be challenged. Appointments may be delayed. Funding may be withheld. Authority may be questioned.

To the impatient, this can look like dysfunction.

Sometimes it is dysfunction.

But sometimes it is the system working exactly as designed.

Friction is not always a defect.

In a constitutional republic, friction can be protection.

It slows power down long enough for the people to see it.

It forces argument into the open.

It requires officials to justify action.

It prevents one election, one leader, one branch, one emergency, or one temporary majority from converting preference into command without resistance.

A system without friction may look cleaner.

It may move faster.

It may satisfy the immediate demand for action.

But speed is not the same as freedom.

A train with no brakes is efficient only until it must stop.

Checks and balances are the brakes inside the constitutional system.

They do not exist to prevent all action. They exist to prevent unchecked action.

That difference matters.

The Constitution does not make government powerless. It makes government answerable. It requires public power to pass through more than one institutional gate before it reaches the people with binding force.

That process can be slow.

It can be irritating.

It can produce compromise that satisfies no one completely.

But it also prevents the government from becoming too simple.

Too unified.

Too easy to command.

Too easy to capture.

Too easy to weaponize.

A free people should be suspicious of any political theory that treats constitutional friction as merely an obstacle to progress. The obstacle may be the safeguard. The delay may be the warning system. The disagreement may be the mechanism by which power is prevented from hardening into rule.

The framers knew that liberty required an internal structure of resistance. They had seen what happened when power became concentrated. They understood that written limits alone would not be enough if the branches had no ability or incentive to defend their own boundaries.

So the Constitution gives power the tools to resist power.

Congress can refuse funding.

The President can veto legislation.

The Senate can reject appointments.

Courts can invalidate unconstitutional action.

The House can impeach.

The Senate can try impeachments.

The people can remove officials through elections.

States can resist federal overreach through their own constitutional role.

None of these checks is perfect.

All can be misused.

A veto can be principled or political.

Oversight can be legitimate or theatrical.

Courts can restrain power or exceed their own role.

Impeachment can be necessary or abused.

Confirmation can be deliberative or partisan.

The fact that tools can be misused does not mean the tools are unnecessary. It means citizens must understand them well enough to distinguish constitutional resistance from political performance.

Checks and balances are not meant to produce harmony.

They are meant to produce lawful tension.

A branch that never resists another branch may not be showing maturity. It may be abandoning its duty. A Congress that lets the executive govern by decree is not being efficient. It is surrendering legislative responsibility. A court that defers to every assertion of authority is not being restrained. It may be allowing power to define its own limits. An executive that treats opposition as disloyalty is not leading a republic. It is forgetting that disagreement is built into the system.

The branches are supposed to make each other uncomfortable.

Not recklessly.

Not constantly.

Not for spectacle.

But constitutionally.

The discomfort is part of the design.

It keeps each branch aware that it is not alone in the system. It keeps officials aware that their authority has edges. It keeps citizens aware that no institution is supposed to become the whole government.

The danger comes when the branches stop guarding their functions.

If Congress prefers popularity without responsibility, it may pass vague laws and leave the hard decisions to agencies.

If the executive prefers control without authorization, it may stretch enforcement, emergency powers, or regulatory guidance into substitute lawmaking.

If courts prefer outcomes over constitutional role, they may resolve political disputes by creating meanings the people never adopted.

If agencies prefer permanence, they may grow into bodies that write, enforce, and judge rules under the same roof.

In those moments, checks and balances weaken.

Power no longer collides with power.

It begins to cooperate with itself.

That may sound peaceful.

It is not.

When government power stops resisting itself, the citizen becomes the main object of pressure.

The system was designed so that government would absorb the friction before the people did. Branches would check branches. Institutions would test institutions. Power would encounter power.

If those checks fail, power flows more directly toward the citizen.

That is why the health of checks and balances is not a technical matter for lawyers alone. It is a matter of civic freedom. Ordinary life is affected by whether Congress legislates clearly, whether executives stay within lawful bounds, whether courts interpret faithfully, whether agencies remain accountable, and whether states preserve their role.

Checks and balances are the architecture of humility.

They remind every official that someone else has a claim.

They remind every branch that it is partial.

They remind every movement that victory is not sovereignty.

They remind every majority that desire is not authority.

They remind every institution that the Constitution, not the institution, is the frame.

A constitutional republic requires that kind of humility because no branch can be trusted alone.

The people are not asked to place all faith in one leader.

They are not asked to place all faith in one legislature.

They are not asked to place all faith in judges.

They are not asked to place all faith in experts.

They are asked to preserve a system where power is separated, checked, balanced, exposed, slowed, and made answerable.

That system will always irritate those who want power to move without resistance.

It should.

That irritation is one sign that the structure is still alive.

A government that can do whatever it wants without collision is not operating under constitutional discipline. It may still use constitutional language. It may still hold elections. It may still invoke the people. But the inner architecture has weakened.

The Constitution was built to prevent that.

It was built so power would not glide.

It would have to climb.

It would have to answer.

It would have to persuade.

It would have to survive institutional resistance.

It would have to remain inside the structure.

Friction, in this system, is not merely delay.

It is a form of protection.

It is the sound of power being governed before it governs the people.

7

FEDERALISM

The Constitution does not create one single center of power over the entire country.

It creates layers.

National authority.

State authority.

Local authority.

This division is called federalism, and it is one of the most important structural protections in the constitutional operating system.

Federalism is often discussed as a technical arrangement between Washington and the states. But it is more than administrative organization. It is a constitutional philosophy about where power should live and how close authority should remain to the people.

The framers understood that concentrated national power could become distant, abstract, and difficult for ordinary citizens to influence. They also understood that the states alone could not hold the country together under the Articles of Confederation. The Constitution was their attempt to solve both problems at once.

Create a stronger national government.

But do not erase local sovereignty.

That balance is the essence of federalism.

The national government was given certain enumerated powers necessary for union: defense, foreign affairs, interstate commerce, currency, treaties, and other national functions. But the states retained broad authority over the ordinary governance of daily life.

This division was intentional.

The Constitution does not assume that every problem should be solved nationally.

It assumes that some powers belong closer to the people.

That principle matters because distance changes accountability.

The farther power moves from ordinary citizens, the harder it becomes to influence, understand, correct, or resist. Large centralized systems can become efficient in appearance while also becoming impersonal, insulated, and difficult to challenge. Citizens may know they are affected by policy without knowing who actually made the decision or how to change it.

Federalism counters that drift.

It preserves multiple centers of authority.

It allows states to govern differently within constitutional limits.

It keeps many decisions closer to local communities.

It prevents every political disagreement from becoming a national struggle for total control.

This is one of the hidden benefits of divided sovereignty.

Not every issue has to be decided by one distant authority for an entire continent-sized republic.

States can reflect regional priorities, local culture, economic differences, and distinct policy judgments while still remaining part of the constitutional union. Citizens retain the ability to influence government at multiple levels rather than existing beneath one consolidated administrative structure.

Local accountability is easier when government is closer.

People can attend school board meetings.

They can speak to city councils.

They can organize within counties.

They can influence state legislatures.

They can see the effects of policies more directly.

They can identify decision-makers more clearly.

They can move between states with different approaches.

They can compare systems in practice rather than living under a single mandatory national framework for every issue.

This diversity is not necessarily weakness.

It can be a safeguard against uniform error.

When every decision is centralized nationally, mistakes also become national. A flawed policy imposed from one center affects everyone at once. But in a federal system, states can function as different governing environments. Some approaches succeed. Some fail. Some are revised. Citizens can observe outcomes across jurisdictions rather than being trapped inside a single permanent experiment.

Federalism also reduces the stakes of national politics.

When all meaningful power gathers at the federal level, every election begins to feel existential. Every presidency becomes a battle over the entire direction of society. Every Supreme Court nomination feels civilization-defining. Every national election becomes emotionally unbearable because so much authority has accumulated in one place.

That intensity is not accidental.

It is often a sign that too much power has become centralized.

The more decisions Washington controls, the more every faction believes it must capture Washington at all costs.

Federalism diffuses that pressure.

It says not every disagreement must become national command.

Some issues remain local.

Some remain state-based.

Some belong to communities closer to the people themselves.

This division protects freedom because it prevents political totalization. No single national majority can completely absorb every layer of governance. Citizens retain additional layers of representation, resistance, and self-government.

Divided sovereignty creates breathing room.

It prevents government from becoming one seamless structure of control.

The states themselves also serve as constitutional counterweights. The federal government is not supposed to stand alone above fifty administrative subdivisions. States possess their own constitutional existence, their own political legitimacy, and their own governing authority within the federal system.

This matters because power checks power not only horizontally between branches, but vertically between levels of government.

Federalism creates another layer of constitutional friction.

States may resist federal overreach.

Federal law may preempt state action in lawful areas of national authority.

Courts may resolve disputes between the two.

Citizens themselves may pressure state governments differently than national ones.

This layered system makes total consolidation more difficult.

Again, friction is not always failure.

Sometimes friction is protection.

A government close enough to regulate every aspect of life from a single center is also close enough to dominate every aspect of life from a single center.

Federalism resists that concentration.

It preserves structural pluralism inside the republic.

The Constitution assumes that freedom is safer when authority is divided geographically as well as institutionally.

This does not mean federalism is simple.

There are tensions.

There are conflicts.

There are hard constitutional questions about where national authority properly ends and state authority properly begins. American history contains deep disputes over federal power, state sovereignty, civil rights, commerce, war powers, and constitutional interpretation. Some state actions have protected liberty. Some have violated it. Federal power has at times corrected injustice and at other times expanded beyond proper limits.

Federalism is not a guarantee of virtue.

No structure is.

It is a distribution of authority designed to reduce the danger of centralized domination.

That distinction matters.

The constitutional operating system does not depend on perfection from any single level of government. It depends on division, accountability, competition, visibility, and lawful restraint.

States themselves are also limited by the Constitution. Federalism does not place states above constitutional rights. States cannot violate protections that bind the constitutional order itself. The Constitution creates both national authority and constitutional boundaries around all public power.

But within those boundaries, states retain meaningful sovereignty.

That sovereignty protects freedom because it keeps the citizen from existing beneath one undivided governing force.

A person in Texas does not live under precisely the same local structure as a person in Vermont or California. Communities can develop differently. Policies can vary. Citizens can choose environments more aligned with their values and priorities. This flexibility lowers pressure inside the national system because disagreement does not always require total victory.

Federalism recognizes something deeply human: people in a large republic will not think alike about everything.

They will differ culturally, economically, geographically, religiously, politically, and socially.

A constitutional republic must create enough unity to remain a nation while preserving enough decentralization to allow real diversity of governance.

Federalism attempts that balance.

It creates one country without requiring one centralized authority over every dimension of life.

This is why divided sovereignty protects freedom.

A citizen with only one source of governing authority has fewer places to turn.

Fewer avenues of resistance.

Fewer competing centers of power.

Fewer opportunities for correction.

But a citizen inside a federal system retains multiple relationships:

Local government.

County government.

State government.

National government.

Courts.

Representatives.

Communities.

Associations.

These overlapping structures complicate consolidation.

They make absolute power harder to achieve.

They force authority to remain distributed.

Federalism also preserves an important psychological truth about self-government: people tend to care more deeply about institutions they can still recognize as connected to their lives.

A distant centralized system can begin to feel abstract and untouchable. Citizens may disengage because they no longer believe their participation matters. But local and state systems often remain more visible, accessible, and responsive.

Self-government weakens when citizens feel permanently distant from power.

Federalism pulls some authority back toward the people.

Not perfectly.

Not always successfully.

But intentionally.

The Constitution does not treat all governance as national governance because the Constitution understands something enduring about freedom:

Concentrated power is easier to command.

Divided power is harder to control completely.

That difficulty is not inefficiency alone.

It is protection.

Federalism protects liberty by preventing sovereignty from becoming fully centralized. It keeps government layered. It keeps authority distributed. It keeps political life from collapsing into one permanent national struggle for dominance.

It preserves space.

Space for states.

Space for communities.

Space for local judgment.

Space for citizens to remain participants rather than merely governed populations beneath a distant administrative center.

The constitutional operating system depends on that space.

Because freedom survives more easily when power must remain divided to reach the people.

And when no single authority becomes large enough to forget that the people came first.

FEDERALISM LAYER MAP

Power Should Flow Up. Accountability Should Flow Down.

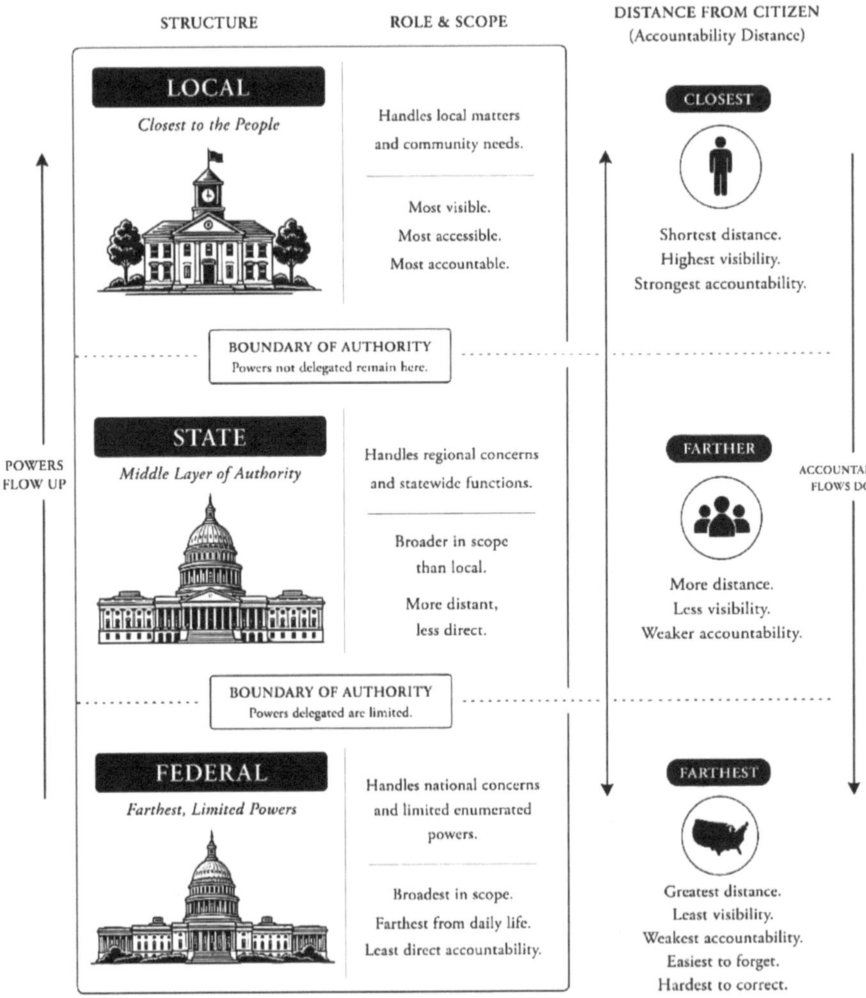

THE FEDERALISM PRINCIPLE

Keep power as close to the people as possible.
As power moves upward, accountability moves downward.
When boundaries blur, liberty suffers.

↑ **POWERS FLOW UP**
Only what is delegated.

↓ **ACCOUNTABILITY FLOWS DOWN**
Always to the people.

★ A FREE NATION DEPENDS ON CLEAR BOUNDARIES AND FAITHFUL STEWARDSHIP. ★

PART III —

THE RIGHTS LAYER

Rights are not permissions. They are the boundary power must recognize.

8

Rights Do Not Come from Government

Rights are not gifts from government.

That is one of the deepest principles in the constitutional operating system.

The Constitution does not treat human freedom as something created by officeholders, agencies, courts, legislatures, or temporary majorities. It treats certain rights as preexisting the government itself.

Government recognizes rights.

It does not create them.

That distinction is not abstract. It changes the entire relationship between citizen and state.

If rights come from government, then rights can be narrowed by government, traded by government, suspended by government, rationed by government, or redefined whenever government decides the public interest requires it.

But if rights exist before government, then government stands in a different position.

It is not the owner of liberty.

It is the institution restrained by liberty.

That is why the Bill of Rights is written largely as a set of prohibitions against government action.

Congress shall make no law.

The right of the people shall not be infringed.

No person shall be deprived without due process.

The language is not the language of permission.

It is the language of restraint.

The Constitution does not say the people may speak because the government allows it. It says government may not abridge speech.

It does not say the people may worship, assemble, keep arms, be secure in their homes, receive due process, or demand a jury because government generously grants those things.

It says public power has boundaries.

The citizen is not free because government is kind.

The citizen is free because government is limited.

This is why treating rights as permissions is dangerous.

Permission implies a superior who may grant or revoke.

A permission-based society teaches people to ask, "Will they let me?"

A rights-based constitutional republic teaches people to ask, "Where did they get the authority to stop me?"

Those are very different questions.

The first question begins with power.

The second begins with liberty.

When people forget that rights do not come from government, they begin to speak as if freedom is something distributed by administrative grace. Speech becomes allowed speech. Worship becomes approved worship. Movement becomes permitted movement. Property becomes conditional use. Privacy becomes what remains after surveillance has made its claims.

The citizen slowly becomes a managed person rather than a sovereign participant in self-government.

The constitutional order resists that inversion.

It says rights are not leftovers.

They are not the spaces government has not yet filled.

They are not privileges granted to compliant citizens.

They are not rewards for good behavior.

They are not favors extended during calm periods and withdrawn under pressure.

They are protections that stand against power precisely when power wants to move.

The rights layer of the Constitution is not decorative. It is defensive architecture.

It protects the person from the state.

It protects the minority from the majority.

It protects dissent from consensus.

It protects conscience from compulsion.

It protects the home from intrusion.

It protects the accused from punishment without process.

It protects the individual from being absorbed into the machinery of government.

This layer matters because even a government created by the people can violate the people.

Popular power is still power.

Majority power is still power.

Elected power is still power.

Administrative power is still power.

Judicial power is still power.

Rights exist because no form of public authority is safe without limits.

The rights layer is where the Constitution says: even here, government must stop.

Even if the goal is popular.

Even if the fear is real.

Even if the public is angry.

Even if officials are certain.

Even if experts insist.

Even if the citizen is unpopular.

Especially then.

Rights are most meaningful when they protect someone the majority does not currently like. A right that protects only approved behavior is not a right. It is permission dressed in constitutional language.

Free speech matters when the speech offends.

Due process matters when the accused is despised.

Search protections matter when officials are convinced they know better.

Religious liberty matters when belief is unfashionable.

Property rights matter when public pressure wants immediate use of what someone else owns.

The right to bear arms matters most when the state would prefer dependent citizens.

The right to a jury matters when the government wants punishment to move quickly.

Rights slow power down.

That is their function.

They force government to justify itself.

They prevent urgency from becoming command.

They preserve the dignity of the person against the appetite of the institution.

The Constitution's rights layer also reminds us that the individual is not merely a unit inside a collective project. A person has boundaries. A person has conscience. A person has speech, property, privacy, body, belief, defense, process, and lawful standing.

Government may regulate in certain lawful ways, but it may not erase the person into the state.

This is one of the places where the Constitution's view of human beings is most visible.

The citizen is not owned.

The citizen is not merely administered.

The citizen is not raw material for policy.

The citizen is a rights-bearing person whose liberties do not originate in government permission.

That does not mean rights have no limits. Constitutional rights exist inside a legal system, and disputes about scope, conflict, application, and interpretation are inevitable. Rights may be balanced against other rights.

Government may sometimes act within lawful boundaries. Courts may define standards. Legislatures may legislate within constitutional limits.

But limits on rights are not the same as government ownership of rights.

A right can have legal boundaries without becoming a government-created privilege.

That distinction must be protected.

Once people begin speaking of rights as though they are granted by government, the burden shifts. The citizen must explain why liberty should be allowed. Government no longer has to explain why restriction is justified.

That is the wrong direction.

In the constitutional operating system, power must explain itself to liberty.

Liberty does not begin by apologizing to power.

The danger of treating rights as permissions is that citizens may gradually internalize subordination. They may wait to be allowed. They may ask whether their freedoms are currently acceptable. They may become grateful for what should never have been treated as a favor.

A free people cannot remain free if they lose the grammar of rights.

They must know the difference between "the government gave me" and "the government may not take."

They must know the difference between "allowed" and "protected."

They must know the difference between "privilege" and "right."

They must know the difference between "permission" and "liberty."

This is why constitutional literacy is not merely academic. Language shapes posture. A people who understand rights as inherent stand differently before power than a people who understand rights as administrative allowances.

The Bill of Rights was not added because the people trusted the new federal government.

It was added because many did not.

They wanted explicit protections. They wanted written boundaries. They wanted certain freedoms named so that government would not mistake silence for surrender.

The Ninth and Tenth Amendments sharpen this point. The enumeration of certain rights was not meant to deny others retained by the people, and powers not delegated to the United States were reserved to the states or to the people.

That is the operating logic.

Rights retained.

Powers delegated.

Government limited.

People sovereign.

The constitutional order begins to fail when that order reverses.

When powers are assumed and rights are permitted, the system has been inverted.

The people become dependent on government tolerance.

Government becomes the measure of liberty.

And the Constitution becomes a document cited by power rather than a structure restraining it.

That is not the design.

The design is clearer and more demanding.

Rights do not come from government.

Government exists inside boundaries created to protect them.

The rights layer is the shield between the person and public power.

It is where the Constitution remembers that a free society is not measured only by what government can accomplish, but by what government is forbidden to touch.

Freedom is not what remains after power finishes speaking.

Freedom is the premise.

Government is the limited exception.

And when government forgets that, the people must remember.

RIGHTS vs PERMISSIONS

RIGHTS

Rights belong to you
by virtue of your humanity.
They exist before government.

PROTECTED
Rights are inherent and protected by the Constitution.

PREEXISTING
Rights exist naturally and independently of government.

GOVERNMENT RESTRAINED
Government's role is to protect rights, not grant or take them away.

vs

PERMISSIONS

Permissions are granted
by authority.
They exist at government's discretion.

GRANTED
Permissions are created and given by those in authority.

CONDITIONAL
Permissions come with conditions and can be limited or withdrawn.

REVOCABLE
Permissions can be changed or revoked at any time.

A FREE SOCIETY IS BUILT ON RIGHTS.
A CONTROLLED SOCIETY RUNS ON PERMISSIONS.

9

DUE PROCESS

Due process is the Constitution's refusal to let force come first.

Before punishment, there must be law.

Before deprivation, there must be process.

Before government reaches the person, the person must be given a lawful path to be heard.

That is not a technicality.

It is one of the core protections of a free people.

Due process means government cannot simply decide, accuse, punish, seize, silence, confine, or destroy because it believes it has a good reason. It must move through law. It must follow procedure. It must respect the boundary between accusation and guilt, suspicion and proof, authority and abuse.

Process is protection.

It protects the unpopular person.

It protects the accused person.

It protects the person standing alone against public opinion.

It protects the person who has been labeled dangerous, inconvenient, offensive, disobedient, or disposable.

It protects the citizen from being swallowed by the machinery of the state before the law has done its work.

A society without due process can still have rules.

It can still have courts.

It can still have officials.

It can still have punishments.

But without real process, those things become instruments of power rather than restraints on power.

The Constitution does not trust punishment by mood.

Mood is unstable.

A crowd can be angry.

A community can panic.

A media cycle can demand sacrifice.

Officials can feel pressure to act.

Institutions can decide that someone must be made an example.

The public can mistake accusation for truth and speed for justice.

Due process stands in the way of that impulse.

It says no.

Not yet.

Not like this.

The law must come first.

That is why due process can feel frustrating in moments of fear or outrage. It slows the reaction. It requires evidence. It gives the accused rights. It demands notice. It requires a forum. It insists that government justify itself before it may deprive a person of life, liberty, or property.

That delay is not weakness.

It is civilization.

A constitutional republic does not prove its commitment to justice by punishing quickly. It proves it by refusing to let punishment outrun law.

Panic is not process.

Popularity is not process.

Suspicion is not process.

Official certainty is not process.

Public pressure is not process.

Due process exists because the state has enormous power once it decides to move against a person. Government can investigate. Arrest. Charge. Regulate. Fine. Seize. Imprison. Remove. Exclude. License. Ban. Freeze. Condemn.

The individual is smaller than the state.

Process is what gives the individual standing.

It forces government to slow down, name its authority, present its case, and submit itself to legal limits.

This matters because power often believes it already knows.

It believes it knows who is guilty.

It believes it knows who is dangerous.

It believes it knows what outcome is necessary.

It believes process is delay.

It believes the result justifies the shortcut.

The Constitution does not accept that posture.

It knows that government can be wrong.

Witnesses can lie.

Evidence can be misunderstood.

Officials can abuse authority.

Institutions can protect themselves.

Majorities can target minorities.

Fear can distort judgment.

Political enemies can be recast as threats.

The accused can be innocent.

Due process is not built for a world where government is always malicious.

It is built for a world where government is human.

And because government is human, it must be restrained before it punishes.

Law before force.

That is the order.

When force comes before law, the citizen becomes vulnerable to raw power. When law comes before force, government must justify itself within a system it does not own.

That order protects more than defendants in courtrooms. It protects the entire civic structure.

A people who accept punishment without process have begun to accept government by accusation.

They may support it when the target is someone they dislike. They may excuse it when the issue feels urgent. They may applaud it when officials promise safety. But a power accepted against one person becomes available against others.

Due process is not merely for "them."

It is for everyone who may someday stand alone.

That is why constitutional protections cannot depend on popularity. The most important test of due process is not whether it protects the admired. It is whether it protects the despised.

The person accused of a terrible act.

The person with unpopular views.

The person the crowd wants removed.

The person the institution wants silenced.

The person the government says is dangerous.

The person no one wants to defend.

If due process does not protect that person, then it does not truly protect anyone.

Rights that vanish under social pressure are permissions.

Process that disappears under panic is performance.

Law that bends to popularity is not law in the constitutional sense. It is mood wearing legal language.

The Constitution demands more discipline than that.

It requires a society to pause before punishment.

It requires government to act through defined procedures rather than appetite.

It requires citizens to tolerate the discomfort of process even when they are certain of the desired outcome.

That discipline is hard.

It asks people to separate emotion from authority.

It asks them to understand that justice is not the same as immediate satisfaction.

It asks them to remember that the state must never be allowed to punish first and justify later.

Once that reversal is accepted, the constitutional order has already been weakened.

Due process also protects property.

It protects liberty.

It protects life.

It protects reputation indirectly by requiring legal standards before state action.

It protects the relationship between citizen and government by ensuring that the person is not treated as an object to be acted upon, but as a rights-bearing participant entitled to notice, hearing, and lawful judgment.

This is one of the quiet dignities of due process.

It forces the government to recognize the person.

Not as a file.

Not as a category.

Not as an obstacle.

Not as an enemy.

As a person under law.

The law must speak before force acts.

That is the safeguard.

In an emergency, due process is often the first protection people are tempted to weaken. They say there is no time. They say the danger is too great. They say normal rules were built for normal conditions. They say the accused are not entitled to full protection because the stakes are too high.

But the stakes are always high when government seeks to deprive someone of liberty, property, or life.

That is precisely why process exists.

Rules that apply only in calm moments are not constitutional restraints. They are preferences.

The constitutional operating system is designed for pressure. It is meant to function when fear is loud, when public emotion is intense, when the government insists that ordinary limits are inconvenient.

Due process is one of the places where the system says:

Even now.

Even here.

Even for this person.

Even under pressure.

Law before force.

This does not mean government cannot punish. It means government must prove, proceed, and punish lawfully. A constitutional system does not deny the need for consequences. It denies the right of government to impose consequences without lawful process.

That distinction is the difference between justice and coercion.

A society can become cruel while believing it is righteous.

A government can become abusive while speaking the language of safety.

A majority can become tyrannical while claiming moral urgency.

Due process stands against all three.

It does not ask whether the crowd is angry.

It asks whether the law has been followed.

It does not ask whether punishment would satisfy public emotion.

It asks whether government has authority.

It does not ask whether the accused is liked.

It asks whether the person has been given the protections owed under the Constitution.

That is why due process is not merely procedural.

It is moral structure.

It reflects the belief that a person cannot be crushed by the state simply because the state wants to move. It reflects the belief that government must remain bound even when it claims certainty. It reflects the belief that justice requires form, not just feeling.

Without due process, rights become fragile.

Property becomes conditional.

Liberty becomes negotiable.

Accusation becomes dangerous.

Government becomes judge of its own urgency.

And force begins to replace law.

The Constitution refuses that order.

It places process between the person and the state.

It slows the hand of power.

It protects the accused from the crowd.

It protects the citizen from the government.

It protects the republic from becoming ruled by fear.

Due process is the line that says punishment must not be delivered by mood, panic, or popularity.

It must come through law.

And if the law is not followed, then the power is not legitimate.

Because in a constitutional republic, force does not create authority.

Lawful process does.

10

SPEECH, CONSCIENCE, AND DISSENT

Free speech is not needed for popular thought.

Popular thought already has protection.

It has numbers.

It has approval.

It has momentum.

It has institutions willing to repeat it.

The real test of free speech is whether a person may say what others do not want to hear.

The unpopular sentence.

The dissenting argument.

The inconvenient fact.

The minority view.

The challenge to authority.

The warning spoken before the crowd is ready to listen.

That is why free speech sits so close to the center of the constitutional operating system. A people cannot govern themselves if they cannot speak, question, criticize, persuade, object, and dissent.

Self-government requires speech.

Without speech, consent becomes managed.

Without dissent, power hears only itself.

The Constitution protects speech because it understands that government should not be trusted to decide which ideas are safe enough to be heard. Once public authority gains the power to determine acceptable opinion, the boundary between governance and control begins to disappear.

Government can punish by law.

Institutions can punish by access.

Majorities can punish by pressure.

But the constitutional principle remains: the citizen must be able to challenge power.

That right is not decorative.

It is structural.

A citizen who cannot criticize government is not truly self-governing. A citizen who may speak only within approved boundaries is not exercising liberty. A citizen who must fear punishment for dissent has already been placed beneath power rather than above it as part of the sovereign people.

The right to speak includes the right to disturb comfort.

It includes the right to question official narratives.

It includes the right to criticize leaders.

It includes the right to challenge courts, legislatures, executives, agencies, schools, experts, movements, and majorities.

It includes the right to say no.

Not violently.

Not lawlessly.

Not without consequence in every private relationship.

But without government becoming the final editor of public thought.

Speech and conscience are connected because speech is often the outward form of inward conviction. A person's conscience cannot remain free if public authority can compel him to affirm what he does not believe or forbid him from saying what he believes to be true.

A constitutional republic does not require sameness of mind.

It requires enough freedom for disagreement to remain lawful.

That freedom is uncomfortable by design.

A society that truly protects speech will hear things that irritate it, offend it, anger it, embarrass it, and unsettle its consensus. That is not evidence the protection has failed. That is evidence the protection is real.

Free speech is easy to praise in theory.

It is harder to defend in the moment.

The moment is always where the test appears.

The speaker seems dangerous.

The view seems irresponsible.

The dissent seems harmful.

The challenge seems disloyal.

The timing seems inconvenient.

The majority feels certain.

The institution feels justified.

That is precisely when constitutional protection matters.

Rights that operate only when speech is polite, popular, accurate, convenient, and approved are not rights. They are permissions.

The Constitution does not protect speech because every speaker is wise.

It protects speech because no government is wise enough to own the boundaries of thought.

People can be wrong.

Citizens can be foolish.

Arguments can be bad.

Rumors can spread.

Debate can be messy.

But the cure for a messy public mind is not centralized control of thought. The cure is more responsibility, more argument, more evidence, more courage, more civic maturity, and a citizenry capable of listening without immediately demanding suppression.

A free people must be trusted with disagreement.

If they cannot be trusted with disagreement, they cannot be trusted with self-government.

Dissent is not a malfunction in the constitutional system.

Dissent is system maintenance.

It reveals where power has overreached.

It exposes assumptions.

It tests official claims.

It forces institutions to defend themselves.

It gives minorities a voice before they become invisible.

It allows errors to be corrected before they harden into policy.

It gives citizens a lawful channel for resistance so frustration does not have to become violence.

This is why dissent should not automatically be treated as disloyalty. In a constitutional republic, loyalty to the country may require opposition to the government. Loyalty to the Constitution may require resistance to institutions. Loyalty to truth may require standing apart from the crowd.

The country is not the same thing as the current officeholder.

The Constitution is not the same thing as the current administration.

The people are not the same thing as the majority of the moment.

Dissent protects those distinctions.

It keeps government from merging itself with the nation.

When rulers begin to say that criticism of them is criticism of the country, the constitutional order is in danger.

When agencies begin to treat disagreement as a threat to public order, the constitutional order is in danger.

When citizens begin to demand censorship of views they dislike, the constitutional order is in danger.

When institutions reward compliance more than truth, the constitutional order is in danger.

Free speech is the pressure valve of a free society.

It allows conflict to move through words before it moves through force.

It allows grievances to be aired.

It allows citizens to organize.

It allows abuses to be named.

It allows the powerful to be mocked.

It allows official mistakes to be exposed.

It allows unpopular truths to survive long enough to be tested.

Many things now accepted as obvious once began as dissent.

Many reforms began as unpopular speech.

Many abuses were first revealed by people willing to say what others wanted hidden.

That does not mean every dissenting view is correct.

It means the system must leave room for dissent because the system itself is not omniscient.

A society that suppresses unpopular thought assumes the present consensus has already achieved final truth.

That is a dangerous assumption.

Human beings are fallible.

Governments are fallible.

Institutions are fallible.

Experts are fallible.

Majorities are fallible.

Courts are fallible.

History is full of official certainties later revealed as errors.

Free speech keeps the possibility of correction alive.

It gives truth a chance to emerge from conflict rather than decree.

The constitutional operating system depends on that.

Because once speech is controlled, the other rights become harder to defend. A person who cannot speak cannot effectively object to unlawful search, unjust punishment, corrupt administration, excessive regulation, abuse of emergency power, or institutional drift.

Speech is how the citizen signals that power has crossed a line.

Speech is how the people remember they are not subjects.

Speech is how consent remains meaningful.

Without speech, elections become thinner.

Representation becomes weaker.

Rights become harder to assert.

Public accountability fades.

And government begins to hear only the voices it has permitted.

That is not self-government.

It is managed opinion.

Conscience also matters because a free society cannot be built entirely on external compliance. The state may command outward behavior within lawful limits, but it cannot own the inner life of the person. It cannot legitimately demand that citizens surrender the private ground where belief, judgment, faith, memory, and moral responsibility live.

A person without conscience becomes easier to administer.

A people without conscience becomes easier to rule.

The Constitution protects the space where the person remains answerable to something deeper than the state.

That space matters.

It is where courage forms.

It is where dissent begins.

It is where citizens decide whether to speak even when speech costs them.

Not every cost comes from government. A person may face criticism, disagreement, loss of reputation, broken relationships, or private consequences for speech. Constitutional protection does not mean speech is free from all reaction.

But government power is different.

When the state punishes speech, it does not merely answer an argument. It brings force to thought. It teaches citizens that some ideas are not merely disputed, but forbidden.

That lesson changes a culture.

People begin to self-censor.

They become careful.

Then quiet.

Then obedient.

Eventually they may forget that silence was learned.

The constitutional system resists that path by protecting the citizen's right to speak before power, against power, and outside the boundaries power prefers.

Dissent as system maintenance means the people must tolerate discomfort for the sake of liberty.

They must resist the urge to silence every view that unsettles them.

They must learn the difference between argument and harm, criticism and violence, disagreement and danger.

They must understand that a society can be noisy and still free, but a society made quiet by fear is already losing something essential.

Free speech is not the enemy of order.

It is one of the conditions of legitimate order.

Because order without speech may only be submission.

The Constitution does not ask citizens to be quiet beneath government. It gives them the right to speak as participants in sovereignty.

To petition.

To assemble.

To publish.

To criticize.

To dissent.

To persuade.

To warn.

To refuse the consensus when conscience requires it.

That is not disorder.

That is the operating system of a free people correcting itself.

Speech keeps the system open.

Conscience keeps the person intact.

Dissent keeps power from believing it is final.

A republic needs all three.

Because government that cannot be challenged will eventually confuse itself with truth.

And people who cannot speak will eventually forget they are the source of authority.

11

Property, Privacy, and Personal Boundary

A free person needs protected space.

Not only physical space.

Not only legal space.

Human space.

A boundary between the individual and the state.

The constitutional operating system understands that the citizen is more than a subject to be governed. The citizen is a person with a home, body, papers, possessions, labor, conscience, relationships, and private life. Government may have authority, but it does not have total access.

That boundary matters.

Without it, freedom becomes theoretical.

A person who can be searched without cause, seized without process, watched without limit, dispossessed without restraint, or entered without lawful authority may still be called a citizen, but he does not stand securely before power.

He lives exposed.

The Constitution does not treat exposure as freedom.

It protects the person's space against government intrusion.

The home matters.

Property matters.

Privacy matters.

The right to be secure matters.

Ownership matters because it gives a person ground on which to stand. A person who owns nothing, controls nothing, and can exclude no one is easier to manage. Property is not merely material. It is practical independence. It gives the individual a sphere of authority not entirely dependent on government favor.

This is why search and seizure protections are so important.

They are not procedural ornaments.

They are boundary protections.

They tell government that suspicion alone is not enough. Curiosity is not enough. Administrative convenience is not enough. Power must have lawful cause before it crosses into the protected sphere of the person.

The home is not supposed to be treated as an extension of the state.

The citizen's papers are not supposed to be treated as open files for government inspection.

The body is not supposed to be treated as a thing to be handled without law.

Possessions are not supposed to be treated as available to public power simply because public power wants them.

The Constitution places a door between the person and the government.

And it requires government to knock through law.

That image matters.

A free people cannot live under the constant feeling that power may enter whenever it chooses. Privacy is not secrecy. Privacy is the ordinary dignity of being unobserved, unsearched, and unpossessed by the state unless lawful standards are met.

A society that treats privacy as suspicious has already shifted toward control.

A person should not have to prove innocence in order to deserve boundary.

The presumption should run the other way.

Government should have to justify intrusion.

That is the constitutional posture.

Freedom requires protected space because human beings cannot fully think, speak, worship, associate, create, dissent, raise families, build businesses, or develop conscience if every part of life is visible to power.

Surveillance changes behavior.

Intrusion changes behavior.

Uncertainty changes behavior.

People become cautious when they believe they are watched.

They become compliant when they believe they can be inspected.

They become dependent when they believe their property is conditional.

They become quiet when they believe no space is truly theirs.

The constitutional system resists that quieting.

It preserves zones of personal authority.

It says the person is not absorbed into the state.

This principle appears in several places across the constitutional structure. The Fourth Amendment protects against unreasonable searches and seizures. The Fifth Amendment protects life, liberty, and property from deprivation without due process, and requires just compensation when private property is taken for public use. The Third Amendment, often overlooked, reflects a related idea: even soldiers of the government may not simply be quartered in private homes without constitutional limits.

These protections share a common instinct.

The individual has a boundary.

The government may not simply cross it.

That boundary is part of liberty.

It is easy to underestimate this because modern citizens often think of freedom mainly as speech, voting, or political participation. Those are essential. But political freedom becomes fragile if the citizen has no secure place to live, no meaningful ownership, no privacy from government inspection, and no protected zone where personal life can unfold outside public authority.

A citizen needs a home that is not merely a location.

A home is where the individual is not performing for the state.

It is where ordinary life is protected from public reach.

It is where family forms, thought deepens, worship happens, books are read, work is done, private grief is carried, children grow, and the person exists without needing permission to be unobserved.

The home is one of the oldest symbols of freedom because it represents a boundary power must respect.

When the state can enter the home casually, the citizen no longer has a place where liberty begins.

Search and seizure protections therefore defend more than property.

They defend personhood.

They say the citizen is not transparent to government.

The citizen is not a file.

The citizen is not a permanently available object of investigation.

The citizen does not lose dignity simply because the state has capacity.

Capacity is not authority.

This distinction becomes increasingly important as technology expands. Government can know more, track more, store more, analyze more, and infer more than earlier generations could have imagined. The tools change, but the principle remains: the ability to see does not create the right to intrude.

Power must still be authorized.

The constitutional question remains.

Where is the lawful authority?

What limit applies?

What process was followed?

What right is being touched?

Modern technology can make old boundaries feel outdated, but that is exactly why the boundaries matter. Without them, convenience and capability can quietly replace consent and law.

A free society must not confuse technological access with constitutional permission.

Property also protects against dependency. When government controls too much of what people need, people may become less willing to oppose government. If licenses, benefits, permits, accounts, ownership records, land use, professional access, and financial life become too vulnerable to political or administrative pressure, citizens may begin to experience freedom as conditional.

They may still speak.

But carefully.

They may still own.

But insecurely.

They may still dissent.

But at personal risk from systems they cannot see or challenge.

This is why personal boundary is not a small matter.

Boundary is where freedom becomes livable.

The Constitution does not create a society of isolated individuals without obligations to others. It does not deny the existence of community, law, or public need. But it does reject the idea that the person belongs wholly to the state or the collective.

The individual is more than a subject.

More than a voter.

More than a taxpayer.

More than a worker.

More than a data point.

More than a recipient of services.

More than an administrative category.

The individual has a sphere that public power must respect.

The danger comes when government begins to treat personal space as something tolerated rather than protected. A tolerated space can be narrowed. A protected space must be justified before it is invaded.

That is the difference between permission and right.

A person who lives by permission has no secure boundary.

A person who lives under rights can say: this is mine; this is private; this is my home; this is my body; this is my property; this is my paper; this is my space; and government must show lawful authority before it crosses.

That posture is essential to self-government.

Citizens cannot govern power if they have no ground from which to stand apart from it.

They cannot challenge power if power has unlimited access to their lives.

They cannot remain free if every private space becomes a potential extension of public administration.

The constitutional operating system protects freedom by protecting distance.

Distance between the person and the state.

Distance between the home and public intrusion.

Distance between ownership and confiscation.

Distance between privacy and surveillance.

Distance between lawful authority and raw access.

That distance is not anti-government.

It is constitutional government.

It defines proper relationship.

Government may serve.

Government may protect.

Government may regulate within lawful bounds.

Government may punish after due process.

Government may take property for public use only under constitutional conditions.

But government may not own the person.

It may not erase private life.

It may not treat the home as open territory.

It may not make exposure the price of citizenship.

Freedom requires protected space because liberty is not only a public condition. It is also a personal condition. It is the ability to live with some part of the self, the home, the family, the mind, and the work beyond the immediate reach of power.

That protected space is where citizens remain human.

It is where conscience survives.

It is where dissent gathers courage.

It is where families pass down memory.

It is where ownership becomes independence.

It is where privacy allows thought to develop before it is judged.

A society without protected space may still have elections.

It may still have slogans.

It may still use the language of rights.

But the citizen will feel different.

Less secure.

Less rooted.

Less able to say no.

The Constitution protects property, privacy, and personal boundary because a free people cannot live permanently exposed to the state.

They need doors.

They need limits.

They need lawful process before intrusion.

They need ownership that cannot be casually taken.

They need homes that remain homes.

They need private life that is not treated as suspicious.

They need government to remember that service is not possession.

The person is not public property.

The home is not government territory.

The boundary is part of the freedom.

PART IV —

THE FAILURE MODES

A republic rarely loses its structure all at once. It drifts.

12

Institutional Drift

Power does not always expand by announcement.

Often, it expands quietly.

Not through one dramatic seizure, not through one obvious rupture, not through one clear moment when the people can point and say: there, that is where the system changed.

More often, power expands through drift.

A small exception.

A temporary program.

A narrow emergency.

A vague delegation.

A practical workaround.

A new office.

A new rule.

A new interpretation.

A process that begins as assistance and becomes authority.

Institutional drift is one of the most dangerous failure modes in the constitutional operating system because it often appears ordinary while it is happening.

Nothing looks revolutionary.

No one says the Constitution has been abandoned.

The language remains familiar.

The offices remain intact.

The courts still operate.

Elections still occur.

Officials still speak of service, protection, efficiency, necessity, and public good.

But the center of gravity moves.

Power shifts from the visible to the hidden.

From elected branches to administrative structures.

From lawmaking to rulemaking.

From constitutional limits to managerial discretion.

From the people's representatives to systems the people barely see.

That is drift.

It does not always feel like tyranny.

Sometimes it feels like paperwork.

Sometimes it feels like compliance.

Sometimes it feels like expertise.

Sometimes it feels like convenience.

Sometimes it feels like inevitability.

That is why it is so difficult to resist.

Power that expands suddenly can awaken opposition.

Power that expands gradually can become normal before people realize what has happened.

The constitutional operating system depends on visible authority. Citizens should be able to trace power back to its source. They should know who made the rule, where the authority came from, what process was followed, what limits apply, and how the decision can be challenged.

Institutional drift obscures that trail.

The citizen encounters a requirement, a denial, a notice, a license condition, a compliance burden, a funding rule, a guidance document, an administrative standard, or an enforcement threat, but the origin of the authority is difficult to identify.

Was this law?

Was this regulation?

Was this agency interpretation?

Was this informal guidance?

Was this executive policy?

Was this judicial deference?

Was this a condition attached to money?

Was this a decision no elected official had to openly defend?

When ordinary citizens cannot tell where power came from, accountability weakens.

Power becomes present but anonymous.

That is one of the defining features of institutional drift.

Government becomes harder to see at the exact moment it becomes harder to avoid.

The normalization of exceptions is one of the main ways drift occurs.

An exception is created for a special circumstance. The circumstance may be real. The need may be genuine. The action may be defensible. But once an exception is accepted, it creates a precedent of habit. The next exception becomes easier. Then the exception becomes a tool. Then the tool becomes a program. Then the program becomes a permanent feature of governance.

The system does not always return to its prior shape.

Emergency measures remain.

Temporary authorities are extended.

Broad interpretations are reused.

Exceptional procedures become standard practice.

What once required justification becomes routine.

What once seemed extraordinary becomes ordinary.

What once would have alarmed citizens becomes part of the background.

This is how constitutional culture weakens.

Not only through open defiance, but through repeated accommodation.

A free people can lose their instinct for limits.

They can become accustomed to government doing things it was never clearly authorized to do. They can become accustomed to decisions being made far from their reach. They can become accustomed to rules arriving from offices they did not elect, through processes they do not understand, under authority no one has clearly explained.

And because life is busy, people adapt.

They comply.

They fill out the forms.

They accept the condition.

They pay the fee.

They change behavior.

They assume someone must have had authority.

Over time, assumption replaces consent.

That is institutional drift.

It converts constitutional questions into administrative habits.

The bureaucracy plays a central role in this failure mode because bureaucracy can become hidden operating code.

A constitution is the visible operating system.

It states the structure.

It names the branches.

It allocates powers.

It protects rights.

It gives the people a framework they can read.

But bureaucracy can become the code that actually runs daily life.

Not always unlawfully.

Not always maliciously.

Not always incompetently.

But often invisibly.

Administrative systems translate broad laws into detailed rules. They define standards. They create processes. They decide eligibility. They issue guidance. They gather data. They conduct enforcement. They shape the practical experience of citizenship.

That work may be necessary in a modern society.

The danger is not administration itself.

The danger is administration without clear accountability, constitutional humility, or meaningful constraint.

When bureaucracy becomes the hidden operating code, the people may still live under the Constitution formally while experiencing government through administrative commands practically.

The Constitution says power is divided.

The bureaucracy may combine functions.

The Constitution says laws are made by elected representatives.

The bureaucracy may create rules with the force of law.

The Constitution says courts judge.

The bureaucracy may adjudicate within its own structures.

The Constitution says rights protect the individual.

The bureaucracy may treat rights as variables inside policy design.

The Constitution says government serves by delegation.

The bureaucracy may behave as though continuity, expertise, and administrative mission create their own authority.

This is not always intentional.

Institutions develop instincts.

They protect themselves.

They expand their jurisdiction.

They preserve funding.

They interpret ambiguity in ways that increase relevance.

They resist reduction.

They produce procedures that justify more procedures.

They convert mission into mandate.

Over time, the institution's survival becomes part of the institution's logic.

That logic may not appear in the Constitution, but it can shape reality more than the Constitution does in daily life.

That is why bureaucracy must remain subordinate to constitutional structure.

Expertise is useful.

Administration is necessary.

Complexity is real.

But none of those things create sovereignty.

An expert does not become a lawgiver because the issue is technical.

An agency does not become unaccountable because the field is complex.

An administrative mission does not erase constitutional limits.

A free people may delegate certain tasks to institutions, but they cannot safely surrender the structure that governs those institutions.

Institutional drift often succeeds because it borrows the language of competence.

It says: this is too complicated for ordinary citizens.

It says: elected officials are too slow.

It says: courts should defer.

It says: experts understand.

It says: process would interfere with action.

It says: accountability is less important than management.

There may be fragments of truth in some of these claims. Modern governance does involve complexity. Expertise matters. Some problems require specialized knowledge.

But expertise cannot replace consent.

Competence cannot replace authority.

Efficiency cannot replace legitimacy.

A system can be well-managed and still be constitutionally distorted.

That is one of the hardest lessons for a modern republic.

The failure mode is not always chaos.

Sometimes the failure mode is smooth administration.

A government can function efficiently while drifting away from the source of authority. Rules can be issued. Programs can run. Compliance can be monitored. Data can be collected. Policies can be implemented. The machinery can look impressive.

But if the machinery no longer remains clearly accountable to constitutional structure, the operating system has been bypassed.

The Constitution was designed to restrain visible power.

Institutional drift often hides power inside process.

That makes the citizen's role harder.

It is easier to oppose a king than a form.

Easier to resist a decree than a guidance document.

Easier to identify a lawmaker than an administrative interpretation.

Easier to challenge a command than a condition.

Easier to see force when it wears a uniform than when it appears as a compliance requirement.

But hidden power is still power.

Soft pressure is still pressure.

Administrative burden is still burden.

A condition attached to access may still shape behavior.

A rule no one voted on may still govern life.

Institutional drift teaches the citizen to accept governance without clear authorship.

That is dangerous.

A constitutional republic requires authorship.

Someone must be responsible.

Someone must be answerable.

Power must not be able to disappear into systems.

The normalization of exceptions, the expansion of administrative discretion, and the quiet shifting of authority all weaken the people's ability to govern power.

This does not happen all at once.

That is why it must be named.

Drift must be seen before it becomes the new ground.

Citizens must ask constitutional questions even when power appears ordinary.

Where did this authority come from?

Who made this rule?

What branch acted?

What limit applies?

Can this decision be challenged?

Is this law, or merely administration pretending to be law?

Is this temporary, or has the exception become permanent?

Is this necessary governance, or hidden expansion?

Those questions are not obstruction.

They are maintenance.

They keep the operating system visible.

They remind institutions that their continuity does not make them sovereign.

They remind bureaucracies that their expertise does not make them constitutional source code.

They remind elected officials that delegation is not escape from responsibility.

They remind courts that deference can become abdication.

They remind citizens that compliance is not the same as consent.

Institutional drift is a failure mode because it changes the system without openly amending it.

It allows power to expand without the people clearly agreeing.

It allows exceptions to become rules without serious constitutional reckoning.

It allows bureaucracy to become the practical code beneath public life.

A free people cannot protect a system they can no longer see.

That is why visibility matters.

That is why accountability matters.

That is why limits matter.

The Constitution was written to make power legible.

Institutional drift makes power foggy.

And fog is where power moves most easily.

INSTITUTIONAL DRIFT

How Clear Structure Becomes Confused Power

1

CLEAR STRUCTURE

The Constitution defines limited powers. Roles are clear. Accountability is direct.

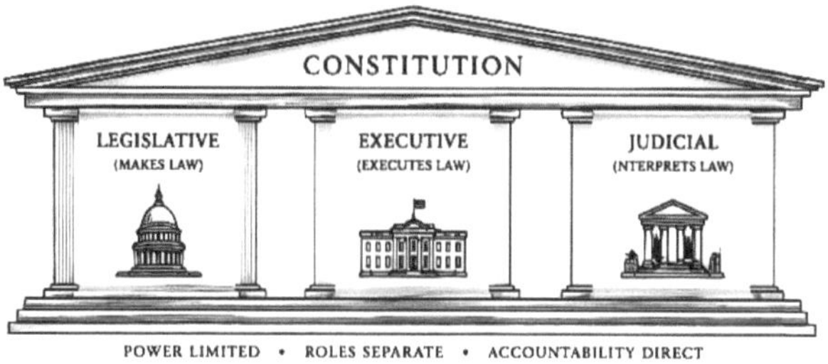

↓

2

BUREAUCRACY OVERLAYS

Agencies, boards, and commissions are added "to help." Layers multiply. Purpose begins to drift.

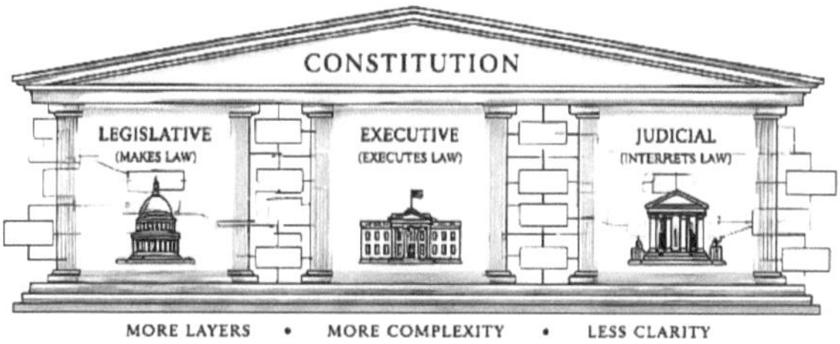

↓

3

FOG LAYERS

Rules, regulations, and interpretations create fog. Visibility decreases. Discretion increases.

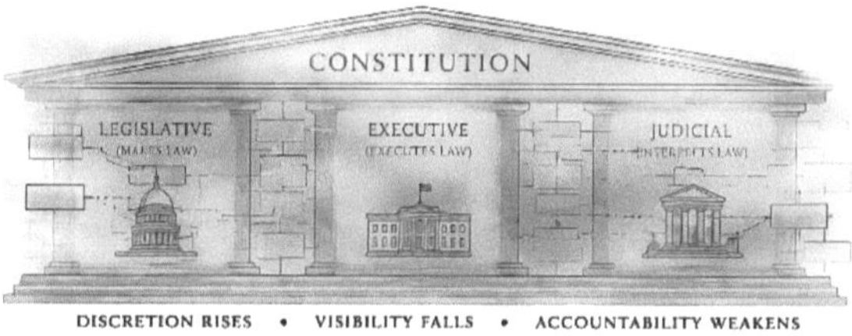

↓

4

BLURRED AUTHORITY LINES

Boundaries fade. Roles overlap. No one is clearly accountable.

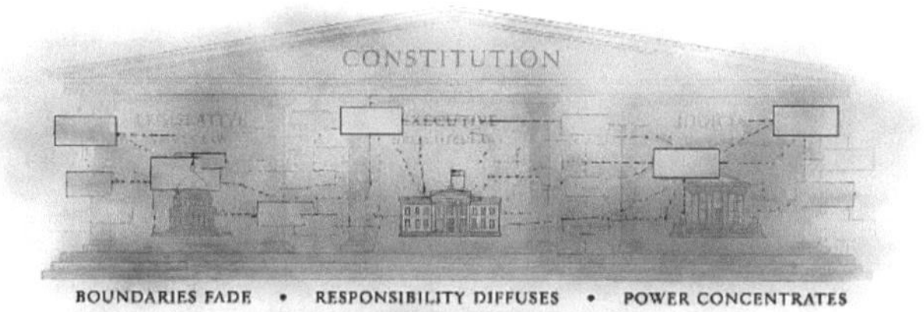

↓

5

INSTITUTIONAL DRIFT

Temporary measures become permanent. Power expands beyond its original limits. Liberty erodes.

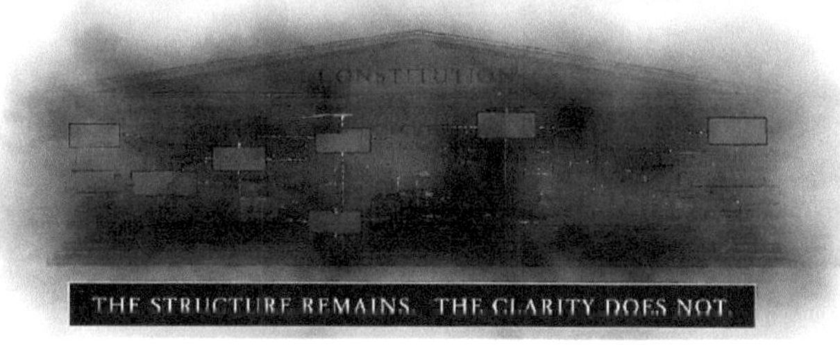

13

EMERGENCY LOGIC

Emergency logic almost always begins with a reasonable sentence.

Just this once.

Just for now.

Just until the crisis passes.

Just because the situation is different.

Just because the normal rules are too slow.

Just because the stakes are too high.

That is why it is so dangerous.

Emergency logic rarely presents itself as hostility to the Constitution. It usually presents itself as necessity. It says the structure is still respected, but not quite suited to this moment. It says rights still matter, but conditions require adjustment. It says procedures still exist, but urgency requires speed. It says limits are still important, but not at the cost of action.

The exception sounds temporary.

The power is not.

Crisis is one of the oldest doorways through which government expands. Sometimes the crisis is real. Sometimes the danger is serious. Sometimes the public is afraid for good reason. The constitutional problem is not that emergencies exist. They do.

The problem is that fear changes the posture of a people toward power.

In calm conditions, people may value limits.

Under pressure, they may demand escape from them.

They may want the executive to move faster.

They may want agencies to act without waiting.

They may want courts to defer.

They may want legislatures to authorize broadly.

They may want speech narrowed, movement restricted, property controlled, privacy reduced, or due process compressed.

They may not experience this as surrender.

They may experience it as safety.

That is why emergency logic is so effective.

It does not always ask people to abandon freedom openly.

It asks them to postpone freedom briefly.

But postponed freedom can become redefined freedom.

Temporary power can become permanent machinery.

Exceptional authority can become normal administration.

A crisis may end, but the precedent remains.

The office remains.

The program remains.

The database remains.

The habit remains.

The legal interpretation remains.

The public's tolerance has been trained.

This is how emergency becomes architecture.

The constitutional operating system was built with a sober understanding of human nature. It does not deny that government must sometimes act with force, urgency, and coordination. A nation must respond to war, invasion, rebellion, disaster, disease, economic crisis, violence, and genuine threats.

But the existence of danger does not erase the need for law.

In fact, rules matter most under pressure.

A rule that applies only when no one is afraid is not much of a rule.

A right that exists only when the public is calm is not much of a right.

A process that holds only when government finds it convenient is not much of a process.

The real test of constitutional structure is whether it remains visible when power has its strongest argument.

That argument is always necessity.

Necessity is powerful because it feels morally superior to restraint. It says delay is irresponsible. It says doubt is dangerous. It says questions are disloyal. It says process is indulgent. It says dissent helps the enemy. It says ordinary constitutional limits were designed for ordinary times.

But a constitution that disappears during extraordinary times has already conceded too much.

The point of structure is not that it prevents action.

The point is that it governs action.

Government can act in emergencies, but it must act through lawful authority, with defined limits, under constitutional accountability, and with a path back to normal order.

Emergency action without boundaries becomes expansion.

Emergency action without expiration becomes permanence.

Emergency action without accountability becomes rule by decree.

Emergency action without rights becomes coercion.

Emergency action without legislative responsibility becomes executive dominance.

Emergency action without judicial scrutiny becomes self-justifying power.

This is why "just this once" must be treated with suspicion.

Not because every request for emergency action is false.

Not because every official is corrupt.

Not because government should be paralyzed.

But because constitutional systems do not usually fail by admitting they are failing.

They fail by creating exceptions that become easier to repeat.

The second exception is easier than the first.

The third feels routine.

Eventually the exception becomes a category.

Then a doctrine.

Then a tool.

Then an expectation.

People begin to ask not whether government has authority, but why government has not already used it.

That is the moment the system has shifted.

Emergency logic trains citizens to prefer force over form.

It teaches them to measure government by immediate visible action rather than lawful discipline. It teaches them that restraint is weakness. It teaches them that those who ask constitutional questions are obstructing relief, safety, justice, or progress.

But constitutional questions are not obstacles to legitimate action.

They are the conditions that make action legitimate.

Where is the authority?

What branch is acting?

What limits apply?

What rights are touched?

What process is required?

How long will this last?

Who reviews it?

How does it end?

Those are emergency questions.

They are not peacetime luxuries.

A free people must ask them when asking them is hardest.

The danger of emergency logic is that it often merges fear with obedience. The citizen begins to feel that questioning power during crisis is morally wrong. The government becomes not merely an institution exercising delegated authority, but the embodiment of safety itself.

Once safety is identified with obedience, liberty begins to shrink.

The constitutional order depends on a different understanding.

Safety matters.

Order matters.

Public action matters.

But safety cannot become the word that allows government to bypass the people, the text, the branches, the rights layer, and the limits that make authority lawful.

A government that can suspend its limits whenever it claims necessity is not limited in any durable sense.

It is limited only until the next crisis.

And there is always a next crisis.

That is one of the hardest truths of political life.

A country will always face something urgent.

War.

Disease.

Terror.

Financial instability.

Civil unrest.

Natural disaster.

Technological threat.

Border crisis.

Crime wave.

Institutional collapse.

Social panic.

The list never ends because human societies are never free from danger. If danger alone is enough to loosen constitutional limits, then constitutional limits are permanently conditional.

The Constitution was not written for a world without danger.

It was written because danger exists, including the danger of government itself.

Emergency logic forgets that second danger.

It sees the external threat clearly, but it becomes blind to the internal threat created when government accumulates power in response.

Both dangers may be real.

A constitutional people must be mature enough to see both at once.

The crisis may require action.

The action may require authority.

The authority must remain bounded.

That is the discipline.

Without that discipline, every crisis becomes a ratchet.

Power moves upward and inward.

It centralizes.

It accelerates.

It bypasses.

It expands.

Then when the immediate crisis fades, the structure rarely returns completely to its former state.

The people may be told that the tools are still needed.

The risk may return.

The system must stay prepared.

The office cannot be dismantled yet.

The emergency authority may be useful for related problems.

The data may help future planning.

The rule may serve another purpose.

The apparatus remains.

This is how crisis becomes permanent expansion.

The constitutional operating system must therefore include memory. Citizens must remember what was temporary. They must ask whether emergency authorities have ended. They must resist the quiet conversion of exception into baseline. They must refuse to let fear rewrite the relationship between the people and the government.

That requires courage.

Not theatrical courage.

Civic courage.

The courage to say the emergency is real, and the Constitution still matters.

The courage to support lawful action while rejecting lawless expansion.

The courage to distinguish necessary government from unlimited government.

The courage to ask for evidence, authority, limits, and expiration when everyone else is demanding speed.

The courage to defend rights for people accused of being dangerous, irresponsible, or inconvenient.

The courage to remember that the system is built for pressure, not only for peace.

Rules matter most under pressure because pressure reveals what rules really are.

If they disappear under strain, they were not rules.

They were preferences.

If rights vanish when unpopular, they were not rights.

They were permissions.

If separation of powers collapses when urgency rises, it was not structural commitment.

It was ceremony.

The Constitution cannot protect a people who treat it as optional whenever the moment becomes intense.

It is either the operating system under pressure, or it is not the operating system at all.

Emergency logic is seductive because it promises relief from difficulty.

The difficulty of process.

The difficulty of disagreement.

The difficulty of limits.

The difficulty of waiting.

The difficulty of lawful authority.

But that difficulty is part of freedom.

A free people do not remain free because nothing frightening happens. They remain free because they refuse to let fear become the new source of power.

The Constitution is not a fair-weather document.

It is a pressure document.

It exists for the moment when government has reasons.

When the crowd has emotion.

When the executive has urgency.

When institutions have confidence.

When citizens are tempted to trade structure for reassurance.

That is when the system must hold.

That is when "just this once" must meet the harder answer:

Not outside the Constitution.

Not without authority.

Not without limits.

Not without process.

Not without accountability.

Not without an end.

Because the emergency may be real.

But so is the danger of power that learns it can expand whenever fear opens the door.

THE POWER EXPANSION PATHWAY

How Temporary Measures Become Permanent Power

1 | EMERGENCY
A real or perceived threat creates pressure for immediate action.

↓

2 | TEMPORARY EXCEPTION
Extraordinary powers are granted as a short-term solution.

↓

3 | ADMINISTRATIVE HABIT
The exception becomes routine. Agencies grow to manage the new power.

↓

4 | NORMALIZATION
The public accepts the new reality. Oversight weakens. Resistance fades.

↓

5 | PERMANENT EXPANSION
The temporary becomes permanent. Power expands beyond its original limits.

FREEDOM SHRINKS NOT ALL AT ONCE, BUT STEP BY STEP.

14

Judicial Substitution

Courts are necessary in a constitutional republic.

But courts are not the Constitution.

That distinction matters.

The judicial branch exists to interpret law, resolve cases, protect constitutional boundaries, and ensure that government remains subject to legal limits. Without courts, rights could become promises without enforcement. Legislatures could exceed authority without consequence. Executives could act without meaningful restraint. Citizens would have fewer ways to stand against unlawful power.

Judicial power is real.

Judicial power is necessary.

But judicial power is still power.

And like every other form of power in the constitutional operating system, it must remain limited.

Judicial substitution occurs when courts stop interpreting the Constitution and begin using interpretation as a substitute for amendment.

That is a failure mode.

The Constitution provides a lawful method for structural change. It can be amended. The process is difficult by design because permanent changes to the constitutional order should require more than preference, urgency, elite agreement, or judicial creativity.

They should require the people, through the constitutional process.

When courts effectively change constitutional meaning without amendment, the people are bypassed.

The change may be praised.

It may be defended as enlightened.

It may be justified as necessary.

It may even produce an outcome many people prefer.

But the constitutional question is not merely whether the outcome is desirable.

The constitutional question is whether the court had the authority to create it.

Interpretation is not the same as rewriting.

Interpretation begins with the text, structure, history, and legal meaning of the Constitution. It asks what the law is. It applies the law to disputes. It gives effect to written limits. It resolves uncertainty while remaining tethered to the source.

Rewriting begins with a desired result and then bends language toward it.

Rewriting treats constitutional text as flexible material.

Rewriting makes the court a substitute for the amendment process.

Rewriting allows five justices, or any judicial majority, to do what the people have not done through constitutional form.

That is not a small shift.

It changes the source of authority.

A court may claim to be protecting rights, advancing justice, modernizing the law, or correcting legislative failure. Sometimes courts have stood courageously against real abuses of power. That role should not be minimized. Courts are essential when they enforce the Constitution against majorities, officials, and institutions that violate it.

But there is a difference between enforcing the Constitution and enlarging it by judicial will.

There is a difference between saying government has crossed a written boundary and inventing a boundary the people never adopted.

There is a difference between applying enduring constitutional principles to new facts and replacing constitutional structure with judicial preference.

That line can be difficult.

But the difficulty does not make the line unimportant.

A written Constitution cannot function as a restraint on power if the branch interpreting it may continually revise its meaning without the people's consent. In that situation, the Constitution no longer governs the court. The court governs the Constitution.

That reverses the order.

The judiciary becomes dangerous when it forgets that it is a creature of the constitutional system, not the source of it.

Judicial independence does not mean judicial sovereignty.

Lifetime tenure does not mean constitutional authorship.

Legal expertise does not mean democratic substitution.

The robe does not create power beyond the text.

The danger of judicial substitution is that it can look respectable. It does not arrive as open defiance. It arrives through opinions, doctrines, balancing tests, evolving standards, broad readings, narrow readings, and legal language that only specialists may fully follow.

The public may experience the result without understanding the method.

A constitutional change appears.

But no amendment was ratified.

No supermajority agreed.

No states consented.

No people deliberated through the structure.

The court simply announced a meaning, and the country changed.

That is a powerful act.

It should be treated as such.

When courts become amendment engines, the amendment process becomes less central. Citizens begin to look to litigation rather than persuasion. Movements seek judicial victory rather than constitutional consensus. Political questions become legal campaigns. The people learn that if they cannot win through the representative process, they may try to win through judicial declaration.

This weakens self-government.

It teaches citizens to bypass one another.

Instead of persuading fellow citizens, building coalitions, changing laws, or seeking amendments, factions seek a court ruling that settles the matter from above.

That may feel efficient.

It may feel morally satisfying.

But it removes the people from constitutional authorship.

A republic cannot remain healthy if the people become spectators while courts revise the operating system.

The amendment process is difficult because the Constitution belongs to the people as a whole, not to temporary institutional majorities. It requires breadth. It requires depth. It requires durable agreement. It forces advocates of change to persuade across states, regions, parties, and generations.

Judicial substitution avoids that discipline.

It can create sudden national rules without the slow work of civic consent.

That can produce backlash, instability, dependence on judicial composition, and a sense that constitutional meaning changes whenever the Court changes.

When that happens, the Constitution begins to feel less like fixed structure and more like contested territory controlled by whoever has the votes on the bench.

That is dangerous for the Court as well.

A judiciary that acts like a political branch will eventually be treated like one.

Its legitimacy depends on the perception that it is applying law, not governing by preference. Once citizens believe judges are merely legislators in judicial form, respect for the institution weakens.

The Court may gain power in the short term while losing authority in the long term.

Authority is not the same as power.

Power can command.

Authority can be trusted.

Judicial substitution threatens both constitutional legitimacy and judicial legitimacy because it makes legal judgment appear indistinguishable from political will.

That does not mean courts should be passive.

A passive court can also damage the Constitution. If courts refuse to enforce clear limits, if they defer to every assertion of emergency or expertise, if they allow branches to exceed their authority, if they treat rights as policy preferences rather than constitutional commands, then courts fail in the opposite direction.

The proper judicial role is not activism or abdication.

It is fidelity.

Fidelity to text.

Fidelity to structure.

Fidelity to limited power.

Fidelity to rights.

Fidelity to the people's authority to amend the Constitution through lawful means.

The court must be strong enough to say no to government.

But restrained enough to say no to itself.

That is the hardest discipline.

Every branch believes it sees something important.

Congress sees political need.

The executive sees urgency.

Agencies see technical complexity.

Courts see injustice, inconsistency, or constitutional conflict.

Each branch can be tempted to stretch its role in the name of solving a problem.

The constitutional operating system demands that each branch remain inside its function even when leaving it would produce a desired result.

For courts, that means interpretation cannot become authorship.

A judge may believe a policy is wise.

That does not make it constitutional.

A judge may believe a constitutional change is morally desirable.

That does not give the court Article V power.

A judge may believe the political branches have failed.

That does not allow the judiciary to become a substitute legislature.

A judge may believe the people are moving too slowly.

That does not make judicial acceleration legitimate.

The people have the right to govern themselves, including the right to deliberate slowly, make mistakes, disagree, persuade, and amend through the process given to them.

Bypassing the people may produce a cleaner answer.

But a cleaner answer imposed without proper authority is not constitutional self-government.

It is substitution.

The Constitution protects freedom not only by announcing rights, but by assigning roles. When courts leave their role, even in the name of rights, the structure weakens. A system cannot remain limited if its guardians become authors of new limits and powers without consent.

The danger is not merely that courts might reach outcomes someone dislikes.

The deeper danger is that the people may forget where constitutional change is supposed to come from.

Not from judicial invention.

Not from administrative necessity.

Not from executive urgency.

Not from legislative evasion.

From the Constitution itself, through the means it provides.

Judicial interpretation is essential because written law must be applied. But interpretation must remain tethered. It must be able to say, "This is what the law means," not merely, "This is what we believe the law should become."

The difference is the difference between judging and governing.

The judiciary is a guardian of the operating system.

It is not an amendment engine.

When courts become amendment engines, they bypass the people.

When they bypass the people, they weaken the source of constitutional authority.

And when the source is weakened, the entire system begins to drift from self-government toward rule by institutional interpretation.

CONSTITUTIONAL AMENDMENT DISCIPLINE

Two Paths. Two Outcomes.

THE CONSTITUTIONAL PATH

Deliberate. Difficult. Durable.

1. PEOPLE → 2. STATES → 3. RATIFICATION → 4. AMENDMENT

1. PEOPLE

The people identify a need for change. The idea is debated and refined.

2. STATES

A proposed amendment is approved by two-thirds of both Houses of Congress and sent to the states.

3. RATIFICATION

The amendment must be ratified by three-fourths of the states through their legislatures or conventions.

4. AMENDMENT

Once ratified, the amendment becomes part of the Constitution for the entire nation.

This path protects the people. It ensures that fundamental change is rare, deliberate, and rooted in national consensus.

VS.

THE JUDICIAL SUBSTITUTION PATH

Quick. Easy. Dangerous.

1. COURT → 2. INTERPRETATION → 3. IMMEDIATE NATIONAL CHANGE

1. COURT

A case is brought before the court.

2. INTERPRETATION

The court interprets the Constitution to reach a new meaning.

3. IMMEDIATE NATIONAL CHANGE

A single decision instantly changes the law for the entire nation.

This path bypasses the people. It concentrates power, weakens accountability, and redefines the Constitution without consent.

THE CONSTITUTION WAS DESIGNED TO BE AMENDED BY THE PEOPLE, NOT REWRITTEN BY THE JUDICIARY.

15

ADMINISTRATIVE EXPANSION

Administrative expansion is what happens when government grows through process instead of open constitutional choice.

It does not always look like power at first.

It looks like expertise.

Procedure.

Guidance.

Compliance.

Standards.

Licensing.

Forms.

Hearings.

Rulemaking.

Implementation.

But over time, these mechanisms can become a separate governing layer between the people and the constitutional branches that are supposed to answer to them.

This is one of the most difficult modern failure modes because administration is necessary. A large nation requires execution. Laws must be implemented. Public systems must be managed. Technical issues require knowledge. Agencies can serve lawful purposes.

The danger is not administration itself.

The danger is administration becoming a substitute for constitutional accountability.

Rulemaking without direct accountability changes the citizen's relationship to power. The citizen may be bound by rules that no elected representative clearly wrote, no legislature specifically debated, and no ordinary voter can easily trace back to a responsible decision-maker.

The rule exists.

The burden is real.

The penalty may be real.

The compliance obligation may be real.

But the authorship is distant.

That distance matters.

In the constitutional operating system, lawmaking belongs to the legislative branch because lawmaking is one of the clearest exercises of public power. It should be visible. It should be debated. It should be voted on. It should expose elected officials to the people's judgment.

Administrative expansion blurs that line.

Congress may pass broad statutes.

Agencies may fill in the details.

Those details may become the real law of daily life.

The citizen may experience the agency more directly than Congress, the President, or the courts. The agency issues the rule, interprets the rule, enforces the rule, grants the license, denies the application, imposes the penalty, and explains the process for appeal.

The architecture begins to compress.

Functions that the Constitution separates begin to gather inside specialized institutions.

That is why administrative expansion can feel like governance by specialists.

The specialist may know more about the subject than the citizen. The agency may understand the technical field. The process may be elaborate. The language may be professional. The file may be thick. The rule may be complex.

But expertise is not sovereignty.

A specialist may advise.

A specialist may administer.

A specialist may help execute lawfully delegated tasks.

But a specialist does not replace the people's authority.

When process becomes governance by specialists, citizens can begin to feel that self-government has been moved behind a technical wall. They are told the issue is too complex. The standards are too detailed. The agency has discretion. The public may comment, but the structure is already moving. The decision is explained in terms few ordinary people can challenge.

This changes how power feels.

It becomes less like law and more like inevitability.

The citizen no longer debates the rule as a participant in self-government.

The citizen complies with the system as a managed subject.

That is the danger.

Administrative systems often expand because they solve problems for the political branches. Congress can avoid difficult specifics by delegating broadly. The executive can claim action through agency implementation. Courts may defer because the agency appears expert. Citizens may be too busy or too overwhelmed to challenge each step.

The system rewards delegation.

The more Congress delegates, the less it must own.

The more agencies govern, the more expertise justifies continued authority.

The more courts defer, the more administrative interpretation hardens into practical law.

The more citizens comply, the more the structure feels settled.

Expansion becomes normal.

And because administrative expansion is often incremental, it rarely forces a single decisive confrontation.

Instead, citizens encounter it one rule at a time.

One license.

One filing.

One reporting requirement.

One compliance standard.

One enforcement letter.

One eligibility condition.

One advisory opinion.

One internal policy.

Each may seem small.

Together they can form an operating system beneath the operating system.

That hidden system may determine how businesses function, how schools operate, how property is used, how speech is regulated indirectly, how professions are licensed, how money moves, how healthcare is delivered, how families interact with institutions, and how citizens experience government in ordinary life.

The Constitution remains visible at the top.

But administration touches the ground.

This is why distance between citizens and power is so important. A citizen can vote against a legislator. A citizen can oppose a president. A citizen can criticize a court. But an agency rule may be harder to reach. The official may be unelected. The process may be opaque. The appeal may require lawyers. The standard may be buried in technical language. The penalty may arrive faster than the remedy.

Distance weakens accountability.

And when accountability weakens, power expands more easily.

The constitutional problem is not that citizens dislike rules. A free society requires rules. The problem is when rules acquire the force of law without the visibility, responsibility, and restraint that constitutional lawmaking requires.

A republic should not be governed mainly by documents ordinary citizens cannot read, processes ordinary citizens cannot access, and decision-makers ordinary citizens cannot remove.

That is not self-government in any meaningful sense.

Administrative expansion also alters the posture of rights. Rights can become variables inside regulatory design. Speech may not be banned directly, but platforms, institutions, funding streams, licenses, or compliance systems may be pressured. Property may not be seized outright, but use may be so heavily conditioned that ownership becomes hollow. Privacy may not be formally abolished, but reporting and data requirements may create constant exposure.

Power does not always need to prohibit.

Sometimes it only needs to condition.

That is the subtlety of administrative power.

The citizen is not always told no.

The citizen is told to apply.

To disclose.

To certify.

To comply.

To renew.

To document.

To wait.

To appeal.

To accept terms.

To adjust behavior.

This can be legitimate when tied to lawful authority and proper limits. But it becomes dangerous when the process itself becomes the method of control.

Process can protect.

But process can also govern.

Due process protects the citizen from arbitrary power.

Administrative process can sometimes become the path through which arbitrary power is made respectable.

A thick procedure is not automatically constitutional restraint. A complex rulemaking record does not necessarily create democratic legitimacy. A public comment period does not replace legislative accountability. An internal appeal does not always cure the problem of concentrated administrative authority.

The question remains:

Who is governing?

Under what authority?

With what limits?

Answerable to whom?

Administrative expansion becomes a failure mode when those questions grow harder to answer.

The people are not supposed to live beneath expert systems they cannot meaningfully challenge. They may rely on expertise, but they do not surrender sovereignty to it. The Constitution does not create government by credential. It creates government by delegated authority, divided function, lawful process, and accountability to the people.

Specialists have a place.

They do not have the place.

The more complex society becomes, the more tempting it is to let specialists govern through process. Complexity becomes the argument for distance. Distance becomes the excuse for discretion. Discretion becomes the habit of authority. Authority becomes expansion.

That is why constitutional discipline becomes more important, not less, in a complex age.

Modern government cannot avoid administration.

But administration must remain constitutionally subordinate.

Congress must not use agencies to avoid lawmaking responsibility.

The executive must not use agencies to create authority the law did not grant.

Courts must not treat expertise as a reason to abandon judgment.

Citizens must not mistake technical complexity for legitimate power.

A free people must be willing to ask basic questions even in specialized fields.

Was this authorized?

Who decided it?

Can it be challenged?

Is it law or guidance?

Is the agency administering the law or effectively making it?

Are rights being protected or managed?

Is the citizen being served or processed?

These questions keep the constitutional operating system visible.

Administrative expansion thrives when people stop asking them.

The danger is not always dramatic oppression. Sometimes the danger is a slow conversion of citizenship into compliance management. The citizen becomes a file moving through systems. Freedom becomes something navigated by forms. Accountability becomes something buried in procedures. Power becomes something no one person seems responsible for, yet everyone must obey.

That is not the constitutional ideal.

Government may administer.

But it must not disappear into administration.

Rules may be detailed.

But they must remain connected to lawful authority.

Specialists may advise.

But they must not become rulers by process.

The distance between citizens and power must not become so great that self-government becomes a memory.

Administrative expansion is a warning sign that the operating system may be running code the people did not write, cannot read, and did not consent to in any clear constitutional sense.

A free people must not accept that quietly.

They must insist that administration remain a servant of law, not a substitute for it.

16

EMOTIONAL POLITICS

Emotional politics begins when feelings replace structure.

Not when citizens feel deeply.

A free people will always feel deeply about their country, their families, their rights, their fears, their losses, their future, and their sense of justice.

Emotion is human.

Emotion is not the problem.

The problem begins when emotion becomes authority.

When fear becomes law.

When anger becomes process.

When compassion becomes unlimited power.

When popularity becomes constitutionality.

When the mood of the moment becomes more important than the structure designed to restrain it.

That is emotional politics.

It is one of the most seductive failure modes in the constitutional operating system because it often feels morally justified while it is weakening the system. People rarely believe they are attacking constitutional structure. They believe they are responding to urgency, harm, injustice, danger, or need.

They believe the moment requires action.

And sometimes action is required.

But the Constitution exists because moments are not enough.

A moment can be intense and still not be constitutional.

A demand can be popular and still not be lawful.

A policy can feel compassionate and still exceed authority.

A leader can be loved and still be limited.

A majority can be sincere and still be wrong.

That is why popularity is not constitutionality.

The Constitution does not ask whether an idea is trending.

It does not ask whether a crowd is angry.

It does not ask whether a movement has moral intensity.

It does not ask whether a leader has a mandate in the emotional sense.

It asks different questions.

Where is the authority?

What power was granted?

What branch is acting?

What right is affected?

What process is required?

What limit applies?

Those questions can feel cold when the public mood is hot.

But that is why they matter.

The Constitution protects against the weather of the moment.

Weather changes.

One day the public demands punishment.

Another day it demands mercy.

One day it fears speech.

Another day it fears censorship.

One day it wants federal action.

Another day it fears federal overreach.

One day it trusts courts.

Another day it condemns them.

One day it wants a strong executive.

Another day it fears executive power.

If constitutional meaning rises and falls with public mood, the system has no fixed point.

Power will simply follow the emotional current.

That may satisfy people when the current moves in their direction. It will frighten them when it moves against them.

A constitution must be more stable than a crowd.

It must be able to withstand fear, grief, anger, enthusiasm, disgust, panic, and hope.

It must protect the unpopular when the popular are certain.

It must protect the accused when the crowd is angry.

It must protect speech when the audience is offended.

It must protect property when the public wants use of it.

It must protect process when people want punishment.

It must protect divided power when people want action from one decisive leader.

This is not because emotion is worthless.

It is because emotion is not enough to govern power.

Emotions can reveal real pain.

They can signal that something needs attention.

They can motivate reform.

They can awaken courage.

They can move citizens from apathy into participation.

But emotion must enter the constitutional system through lawful form.

It must persuade.

It must legislate.

It must amend.

It must organize.

It must debate.

It must submit itself to structure.

When emotion refuses structure, it becomes dangerous.

It begins to treat limits as obstacles rather than safeguards.

It begins to treat disagreement as cruelty.

It begins to treat process as delay.

It begins to treat rights as privileges for the approved.

It begins to treat opposition as moral failure.

It begins to treat power as acceptable so long as power serves the emotionally preferred outcome.

This is how free people can participate in their own loss of freedom.

Not because they hate liberty.

Because they want something else more urgently in the moment.

Safety.

Justice.

Revenge.

Compassion.

Efficiency.

Recognition.

Relief.

Victory.

Those desires may be understandable. Some may even be noble. But noble motives do not make unlimited power safe.

The Constitution was designed for human beings as they are, not as they imagine themselves to be when they are emotionally certain.

People under emotional pressure are capable of overreach.

Majorities under emotional pressure are capable of cruelty.

Institutions under emotional pressure are capable of self-justification.

Leaders under emotional pressure are capable of expanding power.

Citizens under emotional pressure are capable of cheering for tools they will later fear.

That is why structure must come before mood.

Structure does not eliminate feeling. It disciplines it.

It says: your fear may be real, but the government still needs authority.

It says: your anger may be understandable, but the accused still needs process.

It says: your compassion may be sincere, but power still has limits.

It says: your majority may be large, but rights still protect the minority.

It says: your cause may be urgent, but change must move through lawful channels.

This is the maturity a constitutional republic requires.

A republic cannot survive if every emotional wave is allowed to rewrite the boundaries of power.

It needs citizens who can feel strongly without surrendering structure.

It needs leaders who can respond without exploiting panic.

It needs courts that can interpret law without following public weather.

It needs legislators who can deliberate under pressure.

It needs executives who can act lawfully even when action is demanded loudly.

It needs a people who understand that constitutional restraint is not indifference.

Restraint is often the way a free people prevent temporary feeling from becoming permanent power.

Emotional politics also creates a false moral simplicity.

It divides the world into those who care and those who obstruct.

Those who want action and those who stand in the way.

Those who support the cause and those who must be punished.

But constitutional structure is not lack of care.

Asking whether government has authority is not cruelty.

Demanding due process is not approval of wrongdoing.

Defending speech is not endorsement of every speaker.

Protecting property is not indifference to public need.

Limiting emergency power is not denial of danger.

Preserving federalism is not rejection of national purpose.

A constitutional people must be able to make those distinctions.

If they cannot, emotional politics will collapse every structural safeguard into a moral accusation.

Then the person who says "the Constitution still applies" will be treated as someone who does not care.

That is a dangerous cultural moment.

Because once caring is defined as willingness to bypass structure, the Constitution becomes vulnerable to every emotionally persuasive cause.

The system was not built to prevent citizens from caring.

It was built to prevent caring from becoming command without consent.

The Constitution is a restraint on power, not a restraint on conscience.

Citizens may advocate passionately.

They may organize.

They may protest.

They may write.

They may vote.

They may demand reform.

They may seek amendment.

They may try to persuade the country.

All of that belongs inside self-government.

But the line is crossed when the intensity of belief is treated as a substitute for constitutional authority.

No one's emotional certainty is enough to rule another person.

Not a leader's.

Not a court's.

Not a legislature's.

Not an agency's.

Not a majority's.

Not a movement's.

The constitutional operating system exists to keep power from being driven by emotional weather.

Weather is real.

It affects everyone.

But it is not architecture.

A house built for weather must be stronger than the storm.

A Constitution built for human beings must be stronger than public mood.

That does not mean the Constitution never changes. It can change. It has changed. But it changes through itself, not through emotional pressure alone. The amendment process exists because a free people may decide, through lawful and durable consensus, to alter their governing structure.

That is different from allowing the mood of the moment to become law.

Durable change requires more than intensity.

It requires legitimacy.

Emotional politics often wants immediacy.

The Constitution requires form.

That tension will always exist.

But the tension is part of freedom.

If every urgent feeling could instantly become national power, no liberty would be secure. Every right would be only as strong as the next wave of outrage. Every limit would last only until the next convincing crisis. Every citizen would be protected only when the public mood favored protection.

That is not constitutional liberty.

That is emotional rule.

The Constitution protects against that by standing outside the moment.

It says the structure remains even when the mood shifts.

The rights remain even when the speaker is disliked.

The process remains even when the accused is hated.

The limits remain even when the policy is popular.

The branches remain even when one leader is admired.

The states remain even when national action is demanded.

The amendment process remains even when change is desired.

This is how a free people keep their shape.

They do not deny emotion.

They refuse to let emotion govern power.

Emotional politics is a failure mode because it makes the present feel more authoritative than the Constitution. It turns urgency into permission. It turns popularity into legitimacy. It turns structure into inconvenience.

But a constitutional republic must be able to say:

The moment is intense.

The people are moved.

The issue matters.

And still, the Constitution governs.

That is the discipline.

That is the protection.

That is how a country survives its own weather.

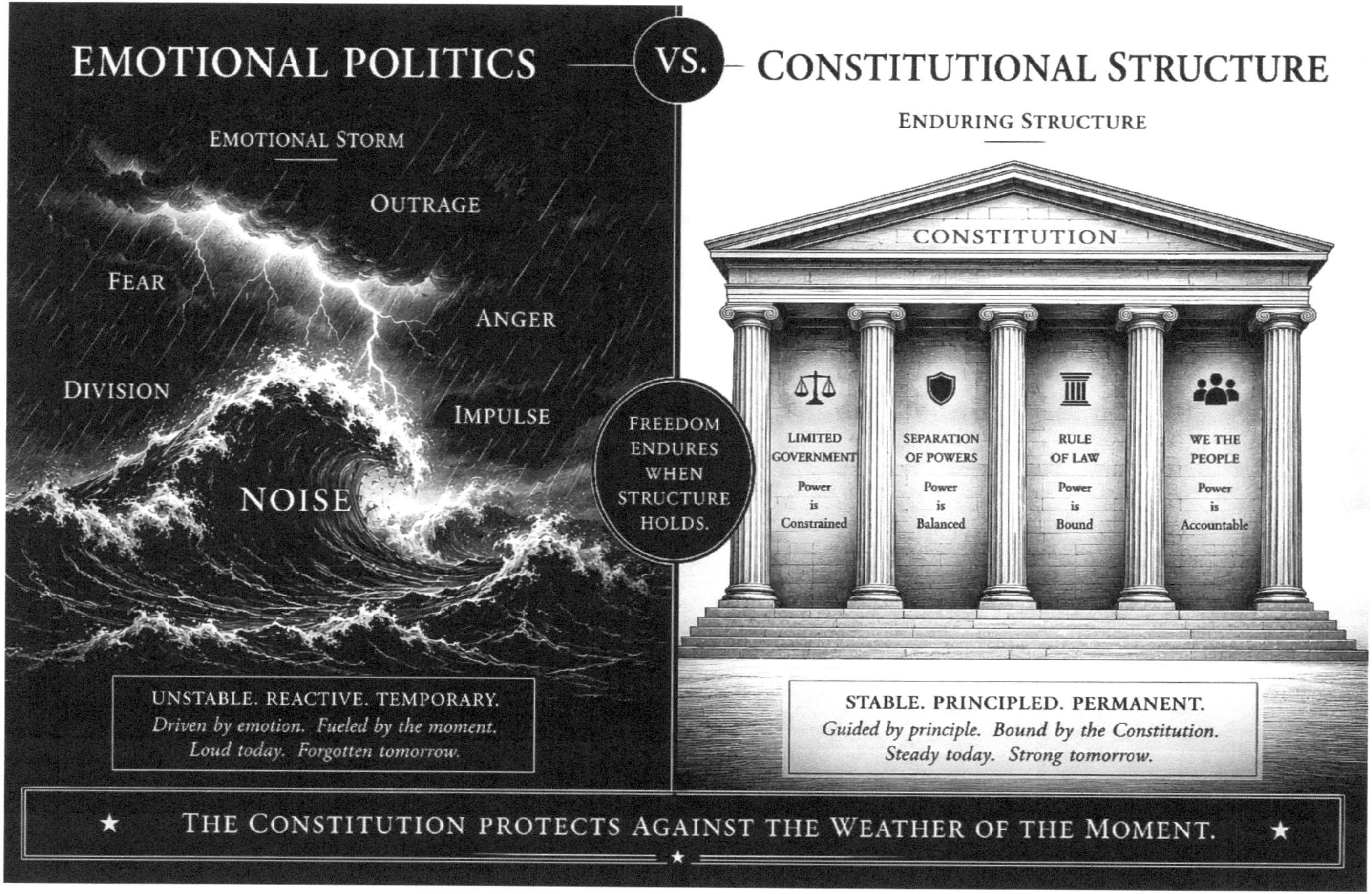

EMOTIONAL POLITICS
VS.
CONSTITUTIONAL STRUCTURE
EMOTIONAL STORM
OUTRAGE
FEAR
ANGER
DIVISION
IMPULSE
NOISE
UNSTABLE. REACTIVE. TEMPORARY.
Driven by emotion. Fueled by the moment.
Loud today. Forgotten tomorrow.
FREEDOM ENDURES WHEN STRUCTURE HOLDS.
ENDURING STRUCTURE
CONSTITUTION
LIMITED GOVERNMENT
Power is Constrained
SEPARATION OF POWERS
Power is Balanced
RULE OF LAW
Power is Bound
WE THE PEOPLE
Power is Accountable
STABLE. PRINCIPLED. PERMANENT.
Guided by principle. Bound by the Constitution.
Steady today. Strong tomorrow.
THE CONSTITUTION PROTECTS AGAINST THE WEATHER OF THE MOMENT.

PART V —

THE AMENDMENT DISCIPLINE

A free people may change the system, but only through the system.

17

THE CONSTITUTION CAN CHANGE — BUT ONLY THROUGH ITSELF

The Constitution is not frozen.

It was never designed to be untouchable.

It can change.

But it can only change lawfully through itself.

That is the discipline.

Article V is the Constitution's repair path. It is the lawful method by which a free people may alter their governing structure without abandoning the structure altogether. It allows correction without collapse. It allows adaptation without rupture. It allows the people to say, through a difficult and deliberate process, that the operating system itself should be amended.

This matters because no human design is complete at birth.

The Constitution emerged from wisdom and compromise, but also from limits, omissions, and contradictions. It required amendment almost immediately. The Bill of Rights was added to make explicit what many believed must be protected from federal power. Later amendments corrected deep failures, expanded citizenship, altered political processes, and adjusted the system across generations.

So the question is not whether the Constitution can change.

It can.

The question is how.

The method matters because method is legitimacy.

A constitutional republic cannot survive if every generation treats the Constitution as binding only until it becomes inconvenient. If the structure can be changed by judicial preference, executive urgency, administrative practice, or emotional public pressure, then the Constitution is no longer the operating system.

It becomes material.

Something to be stretched.

Something to be bypassed.

Something to be reinterpreted until it gives the desired result.

Article V exists to prevent that.

It says: change is possible, but it must be serious.

It must be visible.

It must move through constitutional form.

It must require broad agreement.

It must involve more than a temporary majority, a powerful institution, or the urgency of a moment.

This difficulty is not a flaw.

It is a safeguard.

The Constitution governs more than ordinary policy. It structures the relationship between the people and power. To change that relationship should require discipline, consensus, and durability.

Discipline means the people do not get to confuse preference with amendment.

Consensus means structural change must reach beyond faction.

Durability means the change should be strong enough to outlast the emotion that produced it.

Article V demands that kind of seriousness.

It prevents constitutional change from becoming casual.

Ordinary laws may shift with elections. Policies may change. Programs may begin and end. Budgets may rise and fall. Administrations may govern differently. That is part of political life.

But constitutional amendments are different.

They alter the governing frame.

They are not supposed to be easy because the frame belongs not only to the present majority, but to the entire constitutional people across time.

The dead, the living, and the unborn all live inside constitutional consequences.

That is why amendment must be harder than ordinary politics.

A temporary wave of opinion should not be able to rewrite the permanent structure of power.

A court should not be able to do through interpretation what the people have not done through amendment.

An executive should not be able to do through emergency what Article V requires through consent.

An agency should not be able to do through regulation what the Constitution requires through ratification.

A movement should not be able to do through pressure what the constitutional order requires through lawful form.

Article V protects the people from being bypassed.

It places constitutional authorship back where it belongs: with the people acting through the structure.

That is change without rupture.

A revolution breaks the frame.

An amendment repairs or alters the frame from within.

The difference matters.

A society that cannot change may become brittle.

A society that changes without form may become unstable.

The amendment process stands between those dangers.

It allows the Constitution to remain both fixed and living in the proper sense: fixed enough to restrain power, living enough to be lawfully corrected by the people.

That balance is rare.

Too much rigidity can ignore necessary correction.

Too much flexibility can make the Constitution meaningless.

Article V gives the system a lawful center.

It says the Constitution is not a prison.

But neither is it clay.

It is a structure with its own method of change.

This is the difference between constitutionalism and political desire.

Political desire asks, "What outcome do we want?"

Constitutionalism asks, "By what authority may that outcome be made binding?"

That second question is the discipline of a free people.

It forces citizens to distinguish between what they support and what government may lawfully do. It forces movements to persuade rather than simply pressure. It forces institutions to remain inside their role. It forces time to test intensity.

If an idea is important enough to alter the Constitution, it should be strong enough to survive the amendment process.

That process is not impossible. The Constitution has been amended many times. But it requires breadth because the Constitution is not owned by one faction, one region, one branch, or one generation.

It belongs to the constitutional people.

This is why bypassing Article V is so dangerous.

Bypassing the amendment process may appear efficient, but it changes the source of constitutional meaning. Instead of the people amending their own governing structure, institutions begin amending it for them.

Courts do it through doctrine.

Executives do it through practice.

Agencies do it through accumulated rulemaking.

Legislatures do it through broad delegation.

Public movements do it through pressure that treats resistance as illegitimate.

Each bypass may be defended as necessary. But collectively, they teach the country that the Constitution changes by force of institutional habit rather than by lawful consent.

That weakens self-government.

A people cannot remain sovereign if they are no longer the authors of constitutional change.

The amendment discipline is therefore not only legal.

It is civic.

It requires patience.

It requires persuasion.

It requires restraint.

It requires accepting that not every desired change can be smuggled into the system through interpretation, emergency, or administration.

It requires the humility to say: if we want to change the Constitution, we must do so constitutionally.

That sentence is simple.

It is also demanding.

It denies shortcuts.

It denies emotional entitlement.

It denies institutional substitution.

It denies the belief that urgency alone can create authority.

But it preserves legitimacy.

Legitimacy is what allows constitutional change to endure. A change imposed by judicial creativity may create immediate result but long-term conflict. A change created through emergency may create compliance but not consent. A change created through administrative practice may govern daily life but remain disconnected from the people's authority.

An amendment, properly adopted, carries a different weight.

It has passed through the structure.

It has required broad agreement.

It has become part of the Constitution by the Constitution's own terms.

That is why amendment is not a betrayal of constitutionalism.

It is constitutionalism in motion.

The Constitution's capacity to change through Article V is proof that the system was not built as a closed artifact. It was built as an operating structure with a repair mechanism. But repair is not the same as improvisation. The repair tool is specific. The pathway is defined.

The system can change without breaking.

That is one of its strengths.

A free people should not fear lawful amendment. They should fear unlawful amendment by other means.

They should fear constitutional change that cannot be traced to the people.

They should fear meanings that shift without consent.

They should fear emergency powers that outlast emergencies.

They should fear agencies that rewrite daily life without clear authority.

They should fear courts that become amendment engines.

They should fear executives that treat crisis as permission.

They should fear movements that confuse moral intensity with constitutional legitimacy.

Article V stands against all of that.

It is the discipline of change.

It says the Constitution may be corrected, expanded, refined, and amended, but only through a process serious enough for the gravity of the act.

That discipline protects both liberty and stability.

It protects liberty because power cannot simply rewrite its own limits.

It protects stability because the people know the structure cannot be altered by every passing storm.

It protects legitimacy because change comes through consent, not capture.

The Constitution can change.

But it must change through itself.

That is how a free people repair the system without surrendering it.

18

Why Difficulty Is the Point

The Constitution is hard to amend on purpose.

That difficulty is not a mistake in the design.

It is the design.

A constitution is not an ordinary policy document. It is not a campaign platform, agency rule, executive preference, judicial theory, or temporary expression of national mood. It is the structure beneath those things. It determines how power is granted, divided, limited, checked, and corrected.

Because the Constitution governs the frame itself, changing it should require more than intensity.

It should require seriousness.

That is why amendment is difficult.

Difficulty protects the system from emotional weather. It prevents every popular movement, every political wave, every crisis, every institutional preference, and every temporary majority from rewriting the operating structure of the country.

A free people need the ability to change their Constitution.

But they also need protection from changing it too easily.

That balance is the genius of the amendment discipline.

If amendment were impossible, the Constitution would become brittle.

If amendment were easy, the Constitution would become unstable.

Article V stands between those dangers.

It says change is possible, but it must be earned through broad agreement.

Consensus is legitimacy.

Not perfect consensus.

Not unanimous agreement.

Not the absence of dissent.

But broad, durable, constitutional consensus large enough to show that the change belongs to the people as a whole and not merely to a faction that temporarily gained momentum.

That matters because constitutional change binds people who did not support it. It reaches across states, communities, institutions, and generations. It alters the rules under which future citizens will live. A change of that kind should not rest on narrow passion.

It should rest on serious agreement.

Serious changes require serious agreement because the Constitution belongs to more than the present mood.

It belongs to the country across time.

The living generation has authority to amend it, but not casually. Not by impatience. Not by shortcut. Not by treating opposition as illegitimate. The discipline of amendment forces the people to persuade beyond their own side.

That is healthy.

It requires advocates of change to build a case strong enough to survive disagreement. It requires them to speak across regions, parties, communities, and interests. It requires them to translate conviction into constitutional legitimacy.

That process slows change.

But slowness is not always failure.

Sometimes slowness is protection.

A proposal that cannot survive debate may not be ready for the Constitution.

A movement that cannot persuade broadly may not have the authority to alter the frame.

A cause that depends entirely on emotional urgency may not be durable enough to become permanent law.

The amendment process tests seriousness.

It asks whether the country truly wants structural change, or whether the moment simply feels intense.

That test matters because moments pass.

Constitutional changes remain.

A society governed by immediate feeling will constantly alter its foundations. Each generation, each faction, each emergency, each elite consensus may attempt to inscribe itself into the governing structure.

The result would not be freedom.

It would be instability dressed as progress.

A constitution must have weight.

It must resist easy alteration so that citizens can organize their lives around a stable structure. They need to know that rights do not vanish with the next election. That branches do not shift whenever one party wants advantage. That federalism does not disappear because one national majority grows impatient. That process does not bend every time fear rises.

Durability gives freedom room to breathe.

When the structure holds, citizens are not forced to live under permanent constitutional uncertainty.

They can disagree politically without believing the entire system will be rewritten by whoever gains temporary power.

That stability is part of peace.

It is part of trust.

It is part of ordered liberty.

Difficulty also protects minorities.

If constitutional change could be made by simple majority alone, then rights and structures could be altered whenever enough people became angry, afraid, or ambitious. A minority would live at the mercy of the current public mood. The Constitution would no longer stand above ordinary politics. It would become ordinary politics.

The amendment process makes that harder.

It forces constitutional change to cross a higher threshold than ordinary legislation.

That higher threshold is not anti-democratic.

It is constitutional democracy.

It recognizes that self-government includes both the ability to choose and the discipline to limit how easily foundational rules can be changed.

A free people do not merely vote.

They bind themselves to forms that prevent their own worst impulses from becoming permanent power.

That is maturity.

Difficulty is the point because difficulty forces humility.

It tells citizens: you may be passionate, but you must persuade.

It tells leaders: you may be popular, but popularity is not enough.

It tells courts: you may see a desired outcome, but amendment belongs to the people.

It tells movements: you may be morally intense, but intensity is not legitimacy.

It tells institutions: you may believe change is necessary, but necessity does not erase process.

That humility is one of the hidden virtues of Article V.

It keeps constitutional authorship difficult enough that no single branch, faction, or moment can easily seize it.

It preserves the difference between law and power.

Power wants speed.

Law requires form.

Power wants compliance.

Legitimacy requires consent.

Power wants outcomes.

Constitutionalism requires authority.

The harder path is the constitutional path because the Constitution is not only about getting things done. It is about governing how things may be done.

That distinction is central.

A country can become very efficient after abandoning constitutional discipline. It can centralize authority. It can simplify decision-making. It can reduce disagreement. It can allow institutions to act quickly. It can let experts govern. It can let executives decide. It can let courts revise. It can let agencies manage.

But efficiency is not the same as freedom.

Freedom is often slower.

It requires argument.

It requires persuasion.

It requires distributed authority.

It requires respect for process.

It requires the patience to let legitimacy form.

The amendment process embodies that patience.

It is difficult because the act is serious.

It is difficult because the Constitution is foundational.

It is difficult because the people are not a temporary crowd.

They are a constitutional body.

A crowd can demand.

A constitutional people must consent through form.

That is the difference.

This does not mean amendments should never happen. The Constitution has been amended when the country reached sufficient agreement that the structure itself needed repair. Those amendments matter because they moved through lawful authority. They became part of the Constitution not by institutional improvisation, but by constitutional adoption.

That gives them force.

Not merely political force.

Constitutional force.

They are not just preferred outcomes.

They are lawfully integrated changes to the operating system.

That is what makes amendment different from interpretation, regulation, emergency action, or political pressure.

The difficulty gives the change dignity.

It tells future generations that the country did not merely react. It deliberated. It persuaded. It crossed the threshold required to alter the frame.

Serious agreement does not guarantee wisdom.

No process can guarantee that.

But serious agreement lowers the risk of temporary passion becoming permanent mistake. It gives time for objections to surface. It forces proponents to refine their reasoning. It tests whether a change is broad enough to deserve constitutional status.

A constitution should not be easily captured.

That is the point.

If an amendment is truly necessary, its advocates must build the consent required.

If they cannot, the answer is not to bypass the process.

The answer is to keep persuading.

That is what self-government requires.

The difficulty of amendment protects the people from being governed by impatience. It protects the Constitution from becoming a scoreboard for temporary victories. It protects the system from being reshaped by every political storm.

It also protects future citizens.

Every generation receives the consequences of the prior generation's structural choices. The amendment process asks the present to take that responsibility seriously. It forces the living to remember that they are not writing only for themselves.

They are writing into the architecture of the republic.

That should be hard.

Difficulty is the point because freedom needs a structure that can change without becoming unstable, endure without becoming frozen, and correct itself without surrendering to every pressure that demands immediate power.

The amendment process is not a failure because it is hard.

It is a safeguard because it is hard.

It says the Constitution may be changed, but only when the country has done the work of serious agreement.

And that work is what gives constitutional change its legitimacy.

19

LIVING PEOPLE, FIXED STRUCTURE

A free people can evolve.

They can change their customs.

They can reconsider their laws.

They can build new institutions.

They can face new technologies, new economies, new threats, new forms of communication, and new social conditions.

A constitutional republic does not require a people to remain frozen in time.

But it does require power to remain governed.

That is the distinction.

The people may live in a changing world, but government still needs authority. Society may adapt, but public power still requires limits. Circumstances may become new, but the structure that restrains power cannot be abandoned simply because the moment feels different.

Adaptation is not abandonment.

A living people need a fixed structure precisely because life changes. Without structure, every new condition becomes an argument for new power. Every innovation becomes an excuse for new reach. Every crisis becomes a reason to bypass process. Every social change becomes a justification for treating the old limits as obsolete.

But the danger of power is not obsolete.

Human nature has not been replaced by technology.

Ambition still exists.

Fear still spreads.

Institutions still protect themselves.

Majorities can still be wrong.

Emergencies can still be used.

Language can still be stretched.

Rights can still be treated as permissions.

Government can still forget that it serves.

This is why a fixed constitutional structure remains necessary for a living people.

The Constitution does not answer every policy question for every generation. It was not designed to do that. It gives each generation space to govern, debate, legislate, experiment, amend, and correct.

But it also tells each generation how power must be handled.

Separate it.

Limit it.

Check it.

Enumerate it.

Constrain it by rights.

Submit it to process.

Keep it accountable to the people.

Those principles do not become outdated because the tools change.

A government using digital systems still needs lawful authority.

A legislature facing modern problems still must legislate within constitutional bounds.

An executive responding to new threats still must remain limited.

A court applying old text to new facts still must interpret rather than rewrite.

An agency addressing technical complexity still must remain subordinate to law.

The world may change.

The discipline of power remains.

That is the meaning of adaptation without abandonment.

A free people can apply enduring constitutional principles to new circumstances without pretending that new circumstances erase the principles themselves.

They can regulate new technologies without treating privacy as obsolete.

They can respond to national threats without treating due process as optional.

They can address economic change without treating property as government permission.

They can debate social transformation without treating speech as too dangerous for citizens.

They can reform institutions without turning courts into amendment engines.

They can modernize administration without surrendering self-government to specialists.

The fixed structure is not the enemy of adaptation.

It is what makes legitimate adaptation possible.

Without it, change becomes raw power.

Whoever controls the institution controls the meaning.

Whoever controls the court controls the structure.

Whoever controls the agency controls daily life.

Whoever controls the emergency controls the exception.

Whoever controls the narrative controls the permissible thought.

That is not constitutional evolution.

That is drift.

A constitutional people must be careful with the phrase "living Constitution" if it is used to mean that the Constitution can become whatever a current institution believes it should be. A living people do not need an endlessly shapeshifting Constitution. They need a Constitution stable enough to govern power while flexible enough to be amended through lawful consent.

The living quality belongs first to the people.

They deliberate.

They persuade.

They legislate.

They organize.

They amend.

They correct.

They pass judgment through elections.

They build civic culture.

They teach the next generation.

The structure gives them a lawful way to do those things without turning every disagreement into a constitutional rupture.

That is the gift of fixed form.

It allows motion without collapse.

A bridge is useful because it does not become the river. It lets people cross the river because it holds its shape while water moves beneath it.

The Constitution works in a similar way.

Society moves.

The structure holds.

The people change.

The limits remain.

New facts appear.

Old principles are applied.

The country adapts.

Power is still governed.

If the bridge changes shape with every current, it no longer protects passage.

If the Constitution changes meaning with every political current, it no longer protects liberty.

Fixed structure does not mean no change.

It means change has a path.

Ordinary change happens through ordinary politics.

Statutory change happens through legislation.

Administrative change happens within lawful delegation.

Judicial application happens through interpretation.

Structural change happens through amendment.

Each path has a place.

The failure comes when one path pretends to be another.

When courts amend through interpretation.

When executives legislate through emergency.

When agencies govern through process.

When majorities treat popularity as constitutional authority.

When movements demand structural change without constitutional consent.

That is abandonment disguised as adaptation.

A free people must know the difference.

Adaptation respects the frame.

Abandonment bypasses it.

Adaptation asks how enduring principles apply to new conditions.

Abandonment says the principles no longer bind because conditions are new.

Adaptation keeps the people as the source.

Abandonment transfers authorship to institutions.

Adaptation uses constitutional tools.

Abandonment treats constitutional tools as obstacles.

This distinction is essential to the 250th year and beyond.

A country does not remain free by worshiping its founding as if history ended there. But neither does it remain free by treating its founding structure as a disposable artifact. It remains free by understanding the design well enough to preserve what governs power while correcting what needs lawful correction.

That requires maturity.

The maturity to admit that America has changed.

The maturity to admit that the Constitution can apply beyond the world of its drafting.

The maturity to admit that not every modern pressure creates new authority.

The maturity to pursue amendment when amendment is truly needed.

The maturity to resist institutional shortcuts even when they produce desired outcomes.

The maturity to remain both living and bounded.

A people without fixed structure may feel liberated for a moment. But soon power will find the open space.

Power always does.

It will claim necessity.

It will claim expertise.

It will claim progress.

It will claim safety.

It will claim compassion.

It will claim inevitability.

And without fixed structure, citizens will have fewer ways to answer.

A written Constitution gives them the answer.

Where is the authority?

What does the text say?

What branch may act?

What process is required?

What right is protected?

What limit remains?

What amendment path exists?

Those questions keep a changing people from becoming an unbounded government.

The Constitution does not prevent the people from living.

It prevents power from living beyond its limits.

That is the balance.

The people may evolve.

Power must still be governed.

The country may adapt.

The structure must not be abandoned.

Because a free people do not preserve liberty by letting power change the rules whenever life changes.

They preserve liberty by carrying fixed constitutional discipline into every new age.

PART VI —

THE CITIZENSHIP AS SYSTEM STEWARDSHIP

The Constitution works only when the people remember they are not spectators.

20

THE CITIZEN IS NOT A SPECTATOR

A constitutional republic cannot be preserved by spectators.

It requires citizens.

Not merely residents.

Not merely voters.

Not merely consumers of government services.

Citizens.

People who understand that self-government is not something the government does for them. It is something they participate in, guard, question, and pass down.

The Constitution begins with "We the People" because the people are not outside the system watching it operate. They are the source of the system's authority. If they become passive, the structure weakens. If they stop paying attention, power fills the space they leave behind.

Self-government requires attention.

Attention to language.

Attention to authority.

Attention to process.

Attention to rights.

Attention to the difference between lawful power and convenient power.

Attention to whether officials are serving the structure or using it.

A free people do not need to become constitutional scholars. But they do need enough understanding to recognize when the operating system is being bypassed.

They need to know when a right is being treated as a permission.

They need to know when an emergency has become permanent.

They need to know when a branch is leaving its role.

They need to know when a court is interpreting or rewriting.

They need to know when an agency is administering law or quietly making it.

They need to know when popularity is being confused with constitutionality.

That kind of attention is citizenship.

Citizens are guardians of the system because no institution can fully guard itself.

Congress will not always restrain Congress.

Executives will not always restrain executives.

Courts will not always restrain courts.

Agencies will not always restrain agencies.

Political parties will not always restrain themselves when power is available.

The people must remain awake enough to notice when government begins to forget its place.

Freedom requires participation because power does not stay limited on its own.

Limits must be remembered.

Rights must be asserted.

Processes must be defended.

Questions must be asked.

Elections must matter.

Local institutions must be watched.

Children must be taught.

Speech must be used.

Dissent must remain lawful.

The citizen is not responsible for controlling every outcome. But the citizen is responsible for refusing to surrender the role entirely.

A spectator waits for someone else to fix the system.

A citizen understands that the system depends on him.

Not perfectly.

Not constantly.

But genuinely.

The Constitution does not preserve itself by being admired. It is preserved when people know it well enough to defend its structure under pressure.

The citizen is part of the maintenance layer.

When citizens stop participating, government does not become neutral. It becomes less accountable. Institutions become more confident. Bureaucracy becomes more hidden. Language becomes easier to manipulate. Rights become easier to narrow. Power becomes easier to centralize.

Participation is not only voting, though voting matters.

It is reading.

Questioning.

Speaking.

Teaching.

Serving locally.

Challenging overreach.

Insisting on process.

Refusing emotional shortcuts.

Remembering that the government serves the people, not the other way around.

A free people cannot outsource citizenship and still expect liberty to remain intact.

The system beneath the country requires stewards.

And the first steward is the citizen who remembers: this is ours to keep.

21

CONSTITUTIONAL LITERACY

A free people should know the system they live under.

Not perfectly.

Not academically.

But clearly enough to recognize its shape.

Constitutional literacy is not merely the ability to name the three branches of government or recite parts of the Bill of Rights. It is the ability to understand the operating structure beneath public life.

Where power comes from.

How it is divided.

What limits it.

What rights protect the person.

What process must be followed.

How change lawfully occurs.

Why the people remain the source.

That knowledge matters because a citizen who does not understand the system is easier to govern incorrectly.

Ignorance creates vulnerability.

A person who does not know the difference between a right and a permission may accept permission as freedom.

A person who does not know the difference between delegated authority and assumed authority may accept expansion as normal.

A person who does not know the difference between interpretation and amendment may accept judicial substitution as constitutional change.

A person who does not know the difference between emergency action and permanent power may accept crisis as a new baseline.

A person who does not know the difference between administration and lawmaking may accept bureaucracy as government itself.

This is why constitutional literacy is a form of protection.

It gives the citizen language.

And language matters.

Power often expands by changing language first.

Rights become privileges.

Limits become obstacles.

Dissent becomes danger.

Process becomes delay.

Centralization becomes efficiency.

Surveillance becomes safety.

Compliance becomes responsibility.

Emergency becomes normal.

When people lose constitutional language, they lose the ability to name what is happening.

And what cannot be named is harder to resist.

Structure also matters.

A citizen should know that the Constitution is not merely a list of values. It is a system of roles, boundaries, and procedures. It tells power where to go, where to stop, and how to be corrected.

Without structural understanding, people may judge government only by outcomes.

Did I like the result?

Did my side win?

Did the policy feel good?

Did the leader sound strong?

But constitutional government requires a deeper question:

Was it lawful?

That question is the beginning of civic maturity.

A constitutional republic cannot survive if citizens care only about outcomes and not about authority. The same power used today for a preferred result can be used tomorrow against the people who cheered for it.

Constitutional literacy teaches citizens to think beyond the moment.

It teaches them to ask who holds power, how it was obtained, whether it was granted, whether it is limited, and whether it can be challenged.

It teaches them that process is not empty ritual.

It teaches them that rights are not favors.

It teaches them that federalism is not disorder.

It teaches them that checks and balances are not dysfunction.

It teaches them that amendment is not impossibility, but discipline.

It teaches them that the Constitution is not old paper.

It is the system beneath the country.

Ignorance makes people dependent on interpreters.

They must wait for politicians, commentators, institutions, courts, agencies, or experts to tell them what the Constitution means. Some interpretation will always be necessary. But a people with no basic constitutional literacy can be led almost anywhere by confident language.

They can be told that power has no limit because the cause is urgent.

They can be told that speech is dangerous because dissent is inconvenient.

They can be told that rights must yield because experts have decided.

They can be told that courts may rewrite because politics failed.

They can be told that agencies must govern because the issues are complex.

They can be told that opposition to overreach is extremism.

Constitutional literacy gives citizens a way to pause.

To ask.

To compare the claim against the structure.

To refuse manipulation by mood or authority alone.

A people who understand the Constitution do not become ungovernable.

They become harder to misgovern.

That is the point.

The system requires citizens who know enough to notice when the frame is being bypassed.

Because freedom does not disappear only when force arrives.

Sometimes it disappears when people forget what to call it.

22

The Republic Requires Adults

A republic requires adults.

Not merely people of legal age.

Adults in the civic sense.

People capable of restraint.

People capable of disagreement.

People capable of hearing no.

People capable of losing an argument without trying to destroy the system that allowed the argument to occur.

Self-government is not emotionally easy. It asks citizens to live with delay, limits, compromise, frustration, and outcomes they do not always prefer. It asks them to accept that not every urgent desire becomes law. Not every wrong is repaired immediately. Not every fear justifies power. Not every majority gets to command without restraint.

That requires emotional discipline.

A constitutional republic cannot be governed by tantrum.

It cannot survive if every disappointment becomes proof that the system is broken. It cannot survive if every loss is treated as illegitimate, every limit as oppression, every process as obstruction, and every opponent as an enemy.

The Constitution assumes disagreement.

It does not promise emotional satisfaction.

That is one of its hardest lessons.

The system was built for people who will differ, argue, resist, persuade, organize, and vote. But it also requires them to remain inside the structure while they do so.

That is civic responsibility.

A citizen is allowed to care deeply.

A citizen is allowed to be angry.

A citizen is allowed to demand change.

A citizen is allowed to criticize leaders, courts, laws, agencies, and institutions.

But a citizen in a constitutional republic must also understand that intensity does not create authority.

Feeling strongly is not enough.

Believing oneself right is not enough.

Having the crowd is not enough.

Winning an election is not enough to erase limits.

Losing an election is not enough to abandon the system.

The republic requires adults because freedom requires self-command.

If citizens cannot govern their own impulses, they will eventually invite someone else to govern them.

They will ask for shortcuts.

A stronger executive.

A court that fixes everything.

An agency that bypasses politics.

A national rule that silences disagreement.

An emergency power that moves faster than law.

A leader who does not have to wait.

Every shortcut promises relief from the difficulty of self-government.

But shortcuts have a cost.

They move power away from the people and toward institutions willing to act without the full burden of constitutional discipline.

The discipline of not demanding shortcuts is one of the least glamorous virtues of citizenship.

It means accepting process when process is slow.

It means defending rights when rights protect people you dislike.

It means requiring authority even when you support the outcome.

It means tolerating disagreement without trying to criminalize it.

It means seeking amendment rather than judicial invention.

It means demanding lawmaking rather than executive improvisation.

It means refusing to let fear become permission.

This is adult citizenship.

It does not confuse impatience with courage.

It does not confuse outrage with wisdom.

It does not confuse power with justice.

A republic requires adults because children demand immediate satisfaction. Adults understand consequences.

Children want the answer now.

Adults ask what the shortcut will cost.

Children want the rule changed when they lose.

Adults understand that rules protect them when they are the minority.

Children personalize every disagreement.

Adults preserve the structure that allows disagreement to remain peaceful.

The Constitution depends on that kind of maturity.

It gives citizens enormous responsibility. It does not simply protect them from government. It requires them to become worthy stewards of limited government.

That does not mean citizens must be perfect.

They will not be.

But enough people must remain serious enough, literate enough, restrained enough, and courageous enough to hold the structure when the emotional weather changes.

The republic does not need citizens who feel nothing.

It needs citizens who can feel deeply without surrendering the system.

That is adulthood.

And without it, freedom eventually becomes too difficult for the people who inherited it.

23

RESTORING THE OPERATING SYSTEM

Restoration does not begin with noise.

It begins with structure.

A constitutional republic is not restored by outrage alone, by nostalgia alone, by slogans alone, or by the victory of one faction over another. It is restored when the people remember the design beneath the country and insist that power return to its proper place.

Return to structure.

Return to source authority.

Return to the people.

That is the path.

The constitutional operating system does not need to be reinvented every time the country becomes unsettled. It needs to be understood, honored, repaired where necessary, and applied with discipline. The central problem is not that the Constitution lacks structure. The problem is that citizens and institutions often drift away from it.

Branches blur.

Emergencies expand.

Agencies govern.

Courts substitute.

Rights are treated as permissions.

Citizens become spectators.

Power becomes more comfortable with itself.

Restoration begins when those patterns are named.

Not vaguely.

Not emotionally.

Structurally.

Where has power moved beyond its role?

Where has responsibility been delegated away?

Where has emergency become habit?

Where has administrative process become governance?

Where has judicial interpretation become amendment?

Where have citizens accepted permission in place of rights?

Where has popularity been mistaken for constitutionality?

Those questions are not partisan questions first.

They are constitutional questions.

They return the conversation to the operating system.

A free people cannot restore what they refuse to see. They cannot correct what they cannot name. They cannot govern power if they have lost the language of limits.

Restoration requires recovering that language.

Delegated power.

Enumerated powers.

Separation of powers.

Checks and balances.

Federalism.

Due process.

Rights retained by the people.

Article V.

Consent of the governed.

These are not old phrases for textbooks. They are maintenance tools. They are how the people understand whether the system is functioning or drifting.

To return to structure is to stop measuring government only by whether it produces the desired outcome.

It is to ask whether authority was granted.

Whether process was followed.

Whether rights were respected.

Whether the proper branch acted.

Whether the people remained the source.

Whether the Constitution governed the action, or the action merely used constitutional language after the fact.

A restored constitutional culture does not worship process for its own sake. It understands that process protects substance. It protects liberty. It protects legitimacy. It protects the citizen from being governed by mood, speed, expertise, or force.

Structure is not cold.

Structure is care made durable.

It is how a free people protect themselves even when they disagree.

The second return is to source authority.

"We the People" must become more than ceremonial language.

It must become civic posture.

The government is not the source.

The agencies are not the source.

The courts are not the source.

The parties are not the source.

The experts are not the source.

The people are the source.

Government serves by delegation.

That single idea reorders everything.

It means citizens do not stand beneath public power as managed subjects. They stand before it as the origin of lawful authority. They may obey laws, but they do not belong to government. They may be regulated within constitutional limits, but they are not owned. They may be represented, but they are not replaced.

When source authority is remembered, government must explain itself.

Where did you get this power?

What limit applies?

What right is protected?

What process did you follow?

Who is accountable?

How can the people correct this?

Those questions should not be treated as hostility to government. They are the grammar of constitutional citizenship.

A government worthy of trust should be able to answer them.

The third return is to the people.

Not as a crowd.

Not as a mood.

Not as a demographic category.

Not as a slogan spoken by officials.

The people as constitutional stewards.

The people who read.

The people who question.

The people who vote.

The people who teach.

The people who participate locally.

The people who refuse shortcuts.

The people who defend rights even when inconvenient.

The people who understand that freedom requires more than inheritance.

It requires maintenance.

A republic cannot be restored by waiting for better rulers alone. Better leaders matter, but no leader can replace a constitutional people. If citizens remain passive, even good leaders will not be enough. If citizens remain ignorant, ambitious institutions will fill the space. If citizens demand shortcuts, someone will offer them.

Restoration is not only political.

It is cultural.

It requires citizens who can restrain themselves emotionally, think structurally, and remain loyal to the Constitution even when doing so frustrates their immediate preferences.

It requires adults.

It requires constitutional literacy.

It requires a return to the first principle: the government serves the people; the people do not belong to the government.

This does not mean every conflict disappears. A restored constitutional culture will still argue. It should. Disagreement is not the enemy of the republic. The enemy is forgetting the structure that allows disagreement to remain lawful.

The Constitution was built for conflict.

It gives conflict form.

It gives ambition limits.

It gives dissent protection.

It gives change a path.

It gives power boundaries.

It gives the people a way to govern without becoming either chaotic or ruled.

That is what must be restored.

Not perfection.

Not unanimity.

Not emotional calm forever.

The operating system.

Restoration means Congress legislates instead of evading.

Executives execute instead of ruling.

Courts interpret instead of amending.

Agencies administer instead of governing as hidden lawgivers.

States retain meaningful authority.

Citizens retain protected rights.

Amendments move through Article V.

Power remains visible.

Responsibility remains traceable.

The people remain first.

That is not radical.

That is constitutional.

The difficulty is that drift often feels normal by the time restoration begins. People become accustomed to the new distance between themselves and power. They become accustomed to rules no one clearly authored. They become accustomed to emergencies without endings. They become accustomed to speech being managed, rights being conditioned, and bureaucracy becoming the practical face of government.

Restoration requires noticing what has become normal and asking whether it is constitutional.

That is uncomfortable.

It requires people to stop treating inherited drift as settled law of civic life.

It requires courage to say that the system beneath the country still matters.

Especially when power prefers fog.

Especially when institutions prefer deference.

Especially when movements prefer speed.

Especially when citizens prefer comfort.

But the path is not mysterious.

Return to structure.

Return to source authority.

Return to the people.

Those returns are not backward movement. They are recovery of the operating system that makes forward movement legitimate.

A country can change while remaining constitutional.

It can evolve while remaining bounded.

It can respond to new challenges while still requiring authority.

It can correct injustice without surrendering process.

It can use expertise without surrendering sovereignty.

It can act in emergencies without making emergency the new structure.

It can modernize without abandoning the frame.

But it can only do those things if it remembers what the frame is for.

The Constitution exists to govern power.

If power is not governed, the people eventually are.

That is the final inversion the system was designed to prevent.

Restoring the operating system means refusing that inversion.

It means reminding every institution that it is not the source.

It means reminding every citizen that he or she is not a spectator.

It means reminding the country that freedom is not self-maintaining.

The Constitution still gives the people the architecture.

But the people must keep the architecture alive.

They must read it.

Teach it.

Use it.

Defend it.

Question power through it.

Amend it only through it.

And return to it whenever the system drifts.

That is restoration.

Not a fantasy of the past.

A discipline for the future.

CONCLUSION

Government Under the People

The Constitution is not merely old paper.

It is not a museum artifact.

It is not a patriotic prop.

It is not a collection of quotations for ceremonies, campaigns, courtrooms, and classrooms.

It is an operating system.

A structure for governing power before power governs the people.

That is why it matters.

The Constitution does not assume that liberty survives automatically. It does not assume that leaders remain restrained because they are educated, elected, popular, or well-intentioned. It does not assume that institutions naturally limit themselves. It does not assume that emergencies remain temporary, that majorities remain wise, or that bureaucracies remain small.

It assumes something more realistic.

Power expands unless it is governed.

That is the entire architecture.

Enumerated powers.

Separation of powers.

Checks and balances.

Federalism.

Due process.

Rights.

Amendment discipline.

All of it points toward one central purpose:

To restrain power.

Not eliminate it.

Not paralyze it.

Govern it.

The Constitution creates a government strong enough to function but limited enough to remain accountable to the people who created it. That balance is difficult. It always will be. A constitutional republic is not the easiest form of government. It requires restraint where power prefers speed. It requires process where emotion demands action. It requires limits where ambition wants expansion.

It requires citizens mature enough to preserve a system even when the system frustrates them.

That is why the Constitution works only if the people remember their role.

A constitutional republic cannot survive through institutions alone.

The courts are not enough.

The Congress is not enough.

The presidency is not enough.

No branch can preserve liberty by itself.

The people must remain constitutional people.

People who know where authority comes from.

People who understand that rights are not permissions.

People who recognize that popularity is not constitutionality.

People who insist that emergencies still require limits.

People who can distinguish administration from lawmaking.

People who refuse to surrender structure for convenience.

People who understand that freedom requires participation, discipline, memory, and stewardship.

The Constitution depends on that kind of citizen because the Constitution cannot physically stop power from moving. It has no army of its own. It has no voice except the one citizens give it. It survives because enough people believe the structure still matters.

When they stop believing that, the operating system weakens.

Then shortcuts become normal.

Then exceptions become permanent.

Then institutions begin to govern by habit rather than authority.

Then rights become conditional.

Then the people become spectators.

Then government slowly stops behaving like a servant and begins behaving like a source.

That is the inversion the Constitution was written to prevent.

Government under the people.

Not people under the government.

That principle remains extraordinary.

At 250 years, America is still engaged in the same essential question it faced at the beginning:

Can a free people govern themselves without surrendering to either chaos or concentrated power?

The Constitution was the answer the founders attempted to build.

Not a perfect answer.

But a remarkable one.

A structure strong enough to hold disagreement.

A structure durable enough to survive pressure.

A structure disciplined enough to govern power.

A structure flexible enough to be amended lawfully.

A structure that places the people above the institutions created to serve them.

That structure is not self-maintaining.

It requires vigilance.

It requires literacy.

It requires courage.

It requires adults.

It requires citizens willing to ask constitutional questions even when doing so is inconvenient.

It requires people willing to defend rights they do not personally need at the moment.

It requires restraint when fear is loud.

It requires patience when emotion demands speed.

It requires loyalty not merely to outcomes, but to lawful process itself.

Because once process no longer matters, power becomes the only remaining language.

The Constitution stands against that outcome.

It says power must answer to law.

Law must answer to the structure.

And the structure must answer to the people.

That order must remain intact.

A free people govern power, or power governs them.

There is no permanent middle ground.

Every generation moves the country in one direction or the other.

Toward constitutional self-government.

Or toward administrative, emotional, centralized rule justified by urgency, expertise, popularity, or force.

The choice is never fully finished.

That is why constitutional stewardship belongs to every generation.

The operating system must be remembered again.

Taught again.

Defended again.

Applied again.

Restored again.

Not because the Constitution belongs to the past.

Because it remains one of the clearest attempts in human history to answer a permanent problem:

How do you create government strong enough to function without allowing it to become master over the people?

The American answer was constitutional structure.

Limited power.

Divided authority.

Protected rights.

Law before force.

Citizens before institutions.

Government under the people.

That answer still matters.

But only if the people remember it.

And only if they are willing to govern power before power learns to govern them.

AUTHOR REFLECTION

I did not write this book as a politician, historian, or constitutional scholar attempting to win an ideological argument.

I wrote it as a systems thinker.

Over time, I began noticing the same pattern appearing across institutions, businesses, relationships, finance, technology, education, and government: systems tend to drift when people stop understanding the structure beneath them.

Power expands quietly.

Language changes gradually.

Exceptions become normal.

Process becomes performance.

Citizens become spectators.

And eventually people begin reacting emotionally to outcomes without understanding the operating system producing them.

That pattern led me back to the Constitution.

Not as mythology.

Not as nostalgia.

As structure.

The deeper I studied constitutional design, the more extraordinary it appeared to me. The Constitution is not merely a political document. It is an attempt to solve one of the oldest human problems:

How do you create government strong enough to function without allowing it to become master over the people?

The American answer was not perfection.

It was architecture.

Limited powers.

Divided authority.

Checks and balances.

Rights beyond government reach.

Law before force.

Amendment through discipline.

Citizenship through participation.

What struck me most was how psychologically mature the system assumes the people must become in order to sustain it. A constitutional republic requires restraint. It requires citizens capable of tolerating disagreement, process, delay, and limits even when they strongly desire a different outcome.

That is difficult.

Especially in an age built around immediacy, emotional reaction, algorithmic amplification, and institutional centralization.

Today many citizens experience government primarily through bureaucracy, media narratives, emergency framing, or political identity. The constitutional operating system beneath those experiences often becomes invisible. People know they are governed, but they may no longer know clearly by whom, through what authority, under what limits, or by what constitutional process.

That invisibility creates vulnerability.

This book was my attempt to make the structure visible again.

Not to argue that America has been perfect.

Not to deny historical failures.

Not to claim every constitutional question has an easy answer.

But to recover the operating logic beneath the republic itself.

The people are the source.

Government is delegated power.

Rights are not permissions.

Power must remain divided.

Emergency does not erase limits.

The Constitution can change, but only through itself.

Citizens are not spectators.

These ideas are not abstract to me. I believe they shape whether freedom remains real or slowly becomes procedural language covering institutional expansion.

As America approaches and moves beyond its 250th year, I believe constitutional literacy matters more than ever. Not because citizens need to memorize legal theory, but because free people must understand enough of the system to recognize when it is functioning properly and when it is drifting.

A constitutional republic survives through maintenance.

Through memory.

Through participation.

Through structure.

Through citizens willing to ask difficult constitutional questions even when the emotional pressure of the moment encourages shortcuts instead.

I do not believe the Constitution is self-executing.

It works only if the people remember their role.

That is ultimately what this book is about.

Not worship of government.

Not worship of history.

But stewardship of a system designed to keep power under the people rather than the people under power.

The Constitution remains one of humanity's clearest attempts to build lawful restraint into political authority itself.

I believe that effort is still worth understanding.

Still worth teaching.

Still worth protecting.

About the Author

Lisa J. Scott is an author, attorney, business owner, and systems thinker whose work explores the relationship between structure, sovereignty, freedom, and human responsibility. She is the founder and CEO of In2edge, a consulting firm focused on complex mergers, acquisitions, transitions, and operational execution.

Through her writing, Scott examines the operating systems beneath modern life — from government and finance to education, identity, institutions, and technology. Her books often combine constitutional thinking, systems analysis, philosophy, and lived observation to explore how societies function, drift, adapt, and sometimes lose clarity.

Scott is the author of multiple nonfiction works focused on structure, liberty, self-governance, and modern institutional life, including books on constitutional systems, financial sovereignty, AI and cognitive dependence, education, and organizational design. Her writing style emphasizes clarity over performance and structure over ideology.

She believes constitutional literacy is essential to the preservation of a free society and that liberty survives only when citizens understand the systems governing power around them.

Lisa J. Scott lives in Texas and publishes through Lisa J. Scott Publishing.

Books by Lisa J. Scott

A living body of work

The Core Trilogy

The Woman from Frog Creek

A memoir of origin, sovereignty, and lived refusal.

Following the Compass

On movement, orientation, and learning to trust direction.

The Fixed Point

Stillness, identity, and what remains when motion stops.

Learning & Formation

The Color of Nothing

Lessons on learning, attention, and the space between.

Outside the Bell

A book about children whose intelligence does not ring on cue.

The Bird Who Looked First

A story about early seeing.

The Capsule and the World

How intelligence forms before the world tells it what to be.

Work, Systems & Aftermath

The Art After the Deal

What remains when the transaction is over.

When the Forms Stopped Coming

Short stories from a post–income-tax world.

When Money Changed Quietly

On invisible systems and everyday life.

The First Answer Trap

On thinking with AI instead of stopping at the first reply.

Home, Attention & Everyday Life

The Kitchen Without a Recipe

On cooking, intuition, ingredients, and the intelligence of making.

Relational & Perceptual Works

Rooms of Friendship

On the architecture of relationship.

Borrowed Certainty

On identity formed through inherited belief.

The Mirror Held Twice

Perception, reflection, and seeing again.

The Bright Part

Attention, gentleness, and what draws the eye.

Loving the Idea

On the cost of loving potential instead of reality.

The Shape of Separation

On the quiet architecture of loving what cannot remain.

Mr. Ambiguity

Some people create clarity. Others create weather.

Clarity, Sovereignty & Signal

CLARITY

On clarity as the most valuable asset.

The New Leadership Stack

On clarity, leverage, and proof of work in a changing era.

The Structural Layer

On seeing beyond the story.

The Signal and the Story

On learning to separate what is seen from the story it becomes.

UNSHAkEN

On holding your position when everything else moves.

Operating Systems & Structural Works

The Freedom Stack

A system for building real financial freedom.

Cash Flow is Oxygen

Where financial freedom begins breathing.

Structure Without Walls

On execution, fluid systems, and what holds without rigidity.

The Marriage Operating System

Why love fails without structure.

The Style Operating System

How style becomes consistent through structure.

The Corporate Structure

What org charts hide and systems reveal.

The Creative OS

Where attention becomes structure, and structure protects the signal.

The Aging OS

Where aging becomes structure, and structure protects aliveness.

The Constitutional Operating System

How a free people govern power.

Capstone

The Wayfinder Maps

An integration of the whole.

LISA J. SCOTT
PUBLISHING

www.lisajscottpublishing.com